THE DEACON
AND THE JEWESS:
Adventures in Heresy

THE DEACON AND THE JEWESS:

Adventures in Heresy

by

Samuel Meyer

Philosophical Library
New York

Dedicated to
Esther Lichtenfeld

Contents

Preface

In a study of textual and overt antisemitism why start with Maitland, dubbed "the greatest historian since Gibbon"? As a historian he was not only a contemporary of the dyspeptic Carlyle but the forerunner of Toynbee. These distinguished Britons, when writing of their Jewish compatriots, experience a vertigo which hardly comports with the gravity of their profession and position. Since the crusading blood lust let loose at the coronation of Richard I, the position of the Jew in England deteriorated until the minority of Henry III, the period covered in Maitland's memorable essay on the Council of Oxford which introduced the discriminatory legislation of the Fourth Lateran Council of 1215 into England. The Oxford Council obliged the Jews to wear a distinguishing badge formed of two tablets of stone "lest under cover of a mistake there should be an unholy union of those whom God had put asunder." [1] Edward I found the Jews so impoverished that in 1290 he issued an edict for the banishment of the Jews from England—the first of the great European expulsions. Some enterprising captain expanded his cargo space by depositing his passengers on an offshore ledge which at high tide disposed of his charges. With such a *bon voyage* he was able to complete several round trips a day, increasing the cash flow considerably.

Maitland concluded: "Their expulsion in 1290 looks like the only possible solution of a difficult problem." [2]

In his imaginative and resourceful use of materials, Maitland impressed readers and students with the danger of anachronism. "We must not thrust our modern 'state-concept' upon the reluctant material." [3] G.M. Trevelyan said Maitland used the history of law as a tool to "open the mind of medieval man and to reveal the nature and growth of his institutions." [4] Samuel Roffey Maitland, paternal grandfather of Maitland, who exercised considerable influence upon Maitland, taught in the field of medieval history and wrote, "The past in the present and the present in the past are equally distasteful." [5] In a letter written about his grandfather Maitland wrote: "One has still to do for legal history something of the work which S.R.M. did for ecclesiastical history—to teach men, e.g., that some statement about the thirteenth century does not become the truer because it has been constantly repeated, that a chain of testimony is never stronger than its first link." [6] Near the end of his life Maitland stated that historical-mindedness, far from being the handmaiden of conservatism, is the natural ally of rational reform. He was ever alert to the distorting results of "after-mindedness."

Though armed with historical foresight these tools failed him in the essay here presented. Here is the great puzzle. Our task was an attempt to correct his angle of vision and apply his very teaching to the actual material at hand.

Maitland was seeking the basis for English law which could burn a heretic. The point for us lies in the fact that there was no question in the mind of the council, society and victim that this is good law to be executed as the occasion may warrant.

"No one in England doubted for one moment that this deacon ought to be burnt—every one would agree that this self-made Jew must be burnt, that his death was demanded by all laws human and divine." [7]

In 1847 the English subject James Prescott Joule announced the Law of the Conservation of Energy. His discovery was greeted with violent hostility in a lecture given in Manchester. In Oxford before the British Association for the Advancement of Science, an attempt was made to stifle discussion of the paper which was fortunately frustrated by the enthusiasm of one man in the audience, Lord Kelvin. The oddity of this hostility lies in the fact that the law of thermodynamics is entirely quantitative, a result of physical measurement and its claims are justified by the accuracy of these measurements.

These events, differingly vastly in form and substance, separated by six centuries, both occurred at Oxford, traditional site of enlightenment and gentry. Both reacted to an event with great hostility, moving swiftly to crush the ideas embodied in the challange to tradition.

Maitland gives us the historical sense: "But his crime was enormous; he had piled sin on sin. A deacon of the Christian Church, he had turned Jew, turned Jew for love and for the love of a Jewess." [8]

Both the deacon and Joule, following the paths of their most human interests, acted in a way that offended the values of their times. Established, given values were challenged and the reaction was immediate. Before the Council, no one in England had any doubt that the heretic ought to be burnt. Before the British Association, all save one who had any right to an opinion had no doubt that Joule should be silenced. The deacon who had allowed his love to find fulfillment with a Jewess and altered his religion had, accordingly, committed a heinous offense against the Fourth Lateran Council of Pope Innocent III. Joule tried to reduce a qualitative speculation to a quantative formulation: the hypothesis that heat is a form of energy leading to the principle of the Conservation of Energy now known as the First Law of Thermodynamics. The generally accepted theory up to that time was that heat is a fluid called the caloric which occupies the spaces in a body.

To understand why a mere measurement should provoke animosity on such a scale, we should turn to the work of that earlier scientist Galileo and his experiment with falling bodies and the pendulum. He determined the relationship of the measured time of falling to the measured space, and found that the space traversed is proportional to the square of the elapsed time. This opened the way to the explanation of phenomena on the basis of the equivalence of time, space, mass and motion. He destroyed the fixed value that antique science gave to the qualitative character of final causes and undermined the moral authority of fixed properties. Prior to this event science had consisted of objects connected with values in their relation to man. Knowledge was related to the antecedent reality and moral norm as an end of human destiny.

Qualitative explanations were exploded. Difference in kind between phenomena was abolished and mathematical formulation of equivalence or homogeneity was established. Whether the same emotions rose in the breast of the British Association when Joule destroyed the caloric space theory of heat as arose in the Papal legates who examined Galileo's experiments or the Councillors who sat in judgment on the Deacon, we do not know. But the reaction was identical—abjure the heresy that challenges antecedent morality and fixed and final causes. There is an unparalleled animosity to the scientific method which uses tentative hypotheses and data rather than fixed and unchanging qualities. Intelligence does not pretend to know save as a result of experimentation, the opposite of preconceived dogma.

The goal of physical science has been the subjugation of nature. The preservation of dogma and prejudice are allied to the fear that something old and precious would be destroyed if it were to be opened to the scientific attitude. Yet science is a human extension in our approach to nature in the liberation and enrichment of life.

When Bacon said "Knowledge is power" he meant that knowledge of the laws of nature gives us power to direct the future. The teaching and acceptance of what is already known is the discipline of indoctrination rather than a method of attaining knowledge. The given laws rose under circumstances and conditions that had significance for their time, but as transmuted truths are the dogmas and prejudices of another age.

Determinism, whatever form it takes, is a manifestation of a totalitarian projection of thought. There is one goal, one truth, one orthodoxy. The scientific mind does not pretend to knowledge of these ultimate truths, but tentatively adopts working hypotheses as possible solutions to particular problems. As knowledge uncovers laws, new relationships become operative and forces are freed for the disposal by and use of mankind. The goal of freedom is contained in the process that checks the metaphysics of tyranny and fear. The future lies with those who can use their knowledge to modify existing institutions and devise new ones as a living experiment.

Star-crossed lovers who endure a tragic fate are too numerous to call to attention, but never, I believe, has there been such unanimity evinced on the need for their death. Stephen Langton and the Council were not merely exercising a judicial function, they were executing the will of every person in the Kingdom. If Rousseau's "general will" applies anywhere, it is precisely here.

It is the method of Maitland that must be mastered and applied if we are to understand history and the history of our times. It was Maitland's consistent battle for "historical-mindedness" that shines like a beacon in his life's work. This volume, then, is a tribute to Maitland in his quest for understanding and his abhorrence of anachronism.

S. Meyer
New York City, 1980

xiv

Notes to Preface

(1) *Landmarks of Law,* Ed. Ray D. Henson (Boston: Beacon Press, 1960), p. 251.

(2) Sir Frederick Pollock and Frederic William Maitland, *The History of English Law* (London: Cambridge University Press, 1968), Vol. I, p. 471.

(3) Otto Gierke, *Political Theories of the Middle Age,* tr. introd. by F.W. Maitland (Boston: Beacon Press, 1958), p. IX.

(4) *F.W. Maitland Historian,* Ed. R.L. Schuyler (Berkeley: University of California Press, 1960), p. 3.

(5) Ibid., p. 5.

(6) Ibid., p. 6.

(7) Henson, op. cit. p. 258.

(8) Ibid.

Acknowledgments

The author is grateful for permission to quote brief excerpts from the following:

ANCIENT JUDAISM AND THE NEW TESTAMENT, by Frederick C. Grant. Copyright 1959 by Frederick C. Grant. Reprinted by courtesy of Macmillian Publishing Co., Inc.

CLEMENT OF ALEXANDRIA AND A SECRET GOS-PEL OF MARK, by Morton Smith. Copyright © 1973 by the President and Fellows of Harvard College.

ELDER AND YOUNGER BROTHERS, THE ENCOUN-TER OF JEWS AND CHRISTIANS, by A. Roy Eckardt. Reprinted by permission of Schocken Books Inc. Copyright © 1967 by A. Roy Eckardt.

THE ESSENCE OF JUDAISM, by Leo Baeck. Reprinted

THE DEACON
AND THE JEWESS:
Adventures in Heresy

The Deacon and the Jewess

I

"In the year 1222, Archbishop Stephen Langton held at Oxford a provincial council, and of this council one result was that a deacon was burnt, burnt because he had turned Jew for the love of a Jewess." [1]

Thus opens the remarkable essay *The Deacon and the Jewess; or, Apostasy a Common Law* by that prince of legal historians, Frederic W. Maitland. The problem he tackles is: By what authority and in whose jurisdiction may a heretic be or not be expunged in English law? For this knotty problem he assembles the authorities and whatever statutes, lay and ecclesiastical, he can find to bear on this matter.

It is a sprightly essay in the manner of a club member recalling a school-boy hazing or ragging at this ancient collegium. No tears well up at the tragic episode of this ill-fated love. Garments are not rent nor are ashes strewn on the head. The deacon is not even given a name, nor is the Jewess. No word is mentioned of her trial or punishment, though how such a marked woman could escape the eagle eye of the lord sheriff of Oxfordshire (Fawkes of Breauté) is a mystery best left to Sir Walter Scott.

The men of Oxford were merely endorsing the decrees of the Fourth Lateran Council held by Innocent the Third in 1215. That great lawyer pope "had ordained that Jews and Saracens should wear some distinctive garb, lest under cover of a mistake there should be an unholy union of those whom God had put asunder." [2] "But again we have to ask, whether and why there was anything reprehensible in putting to death this degraded clerk. . . ?" [3] "No one in England doubted for one moment that this deacon ought to be burnt, except, it may be, the deacon himself and his fellow Jews. . . . But his crime was enormous; he had piled sin on sin. A deacon of the Christian Church, he had turned Jew, turned Jew for love and for the love of a Jewess . . . Everyone would agree that this self-made Jew must be burnt, that his death was demanded by all laws human and divine." [4]

If we can break the spell of this enchanting prose for a moment, even for a layman many curious doubts arise from Maitland's account of this case. "In the year 1222 . . ." entones the opening chorale. This is seven years after King John signed Magna Carta. Where is the trial for a capital offense by a jury of his peers? Where is it noted that he had counsel, the right to summon witnesses, cross-examine the evidence? Where indeed is there a law, statute, or precedent binding on a British subject that he could not enter the Jewish faith, marry whom he will? What right of appeal did he have on the facts and the law? His appeal consisted in being burnt at once on the spot.

"The case is good law," says Maitland. "It is a precedent to be followed when occasion shall require." [5] Hannah Arendt remarks: "[One need not] deny the outrageous by deducing the unprecedented from precedents. We need not submit to events as though what in fact happened could not have happened otherwise." [6] By the brute force of its occurrence and being reported, it becomes: ". . . the main, almost the only authority for holding that without help from any statute, English law can burn a heretic, or, at least, an apostate." [7]

But it most certainly was not good law, at least not common law, for Maitland himself observes: "From the death of this deacon until the death of Sautre in 1400 (whether Sautre was burnt under the statute of *that year* or under common law, must not here be asked) no one in England was burnt for heresy—near 200 years." [8] It was (if it was anything but a lynch party) good canon law, in which the executioner acted as the arm of church enforcement. For a common law historian, Maitland was exceptionally appreciative of the canon law. "It was a wonderful system. The whole of western Europe was subject to the jurisdiction of one tribunal of last resort, the Roman Curia." [9]

That there was no English procedure for cases of heresy and apostasy at the time of the deacon's trial is made evident during the reign of Edward II (1307-1327) who, finding no domestic weapons at hand, admitted into England a band of papal inquisitors employing instruments of torture to facilitate the flow of truth.[10]

Maitland, then, was not engaged in a critical examination of history. His is a brief in defense of the *status quo ante*. He would, of course, have warned us against importing modern notions of law into an earlier age. This, he rightly would have regarded as "unhistorical." Yet can the event reported of the Oxford Council be regarded in any way as "law"? All we know from the report written some thirty or forty years after the event, is that a deacon who apostatized for a Jewess had been degraded by the bishop and was at once (statim) delivered to the fire by the lay power.

The writer knows no definition of law which can be reconciled with this event. A society which has attained the conditions of civilization is required to embrace the human goals of honor, love, equality, freedom. Where these are denied or degraded, we have a despotism or mob rule which can in no way be reconciled with any notion of the spirit of law.

Maitland vaults beyond our petty objections: "But his crime was enormous; he had piled sin on sin." Maitland has himself donned clerical robes and the scarlet silks of the bishop.

"No one in England doubted for one moment that this deacon ought to be burnt . . ." "Everyone would agree that this self-made Jew must be burnt, that his death was demanded by all laws human and divine . . ."

Maitland has even discarded the clerical garb and now sits at the Heavenly Throne, in the company of archangels and his Maker and all earthly limitations are transcended, and Divine Judgment, eternal and unalterable, is given.

"The case is good law." That is, good in the sense of "a precedent to be followed."

But Maitland indeed had available for the Oxford Council precedents to follow which might have guided the Archbishop and lord sheriff along different paths.

The son and successor of Charlemagne, the Holy Roman Emperor Louis the Pious (814-840), had a court chaplain, a deacon Bodo. By a curious coincidence this deacon also married a Jewess and converted. (A case which lawyers excitedly refer to as "on all fours.") There is also the precedent of Wecelin, chaplain of Duke Konrad, cousin of Henry II, Holy Roman Emperor (1005), who converted. Andreas, archbishop of Bari, turned from Christianity to Judaism (1078). The priest John, at the end of the eleventh century, living at Oppido, became a Jew.

Christian sources were usually too embarrassed by the subject to mention converts to Judaism, while Jewish sources discreetly avoided the subject. Data on common folk are usually silent, but it is from these dispossessed elements that proselytes were recruited. While Jewish missionary activities were not formally organized, they were not on this account ineffective. "Not only did Jews vie with Christians in attempting to convert the pagan masses, but they also directed their activities towards their adversaries, the Christians." [11]

As for priestly celibacy, though decreed from early times in Rome, the law was greatly neglected in Normandy and Saxon England. In Wales and Ireland clerical concubinage was widespread. The Ecumenical Council of Vienna, 1311, pointed to the brothels at the door of the Pope's palace whose marshals made an income by their upkeep. In the diocese of Coventry a set of canons on incontinency dated 1237 provided that a priest on the first two convictions is to be fined only.

In other words there is a tolerance on the part of the community and this extends to the authorities. The canon law then can scarcely be called binding when broken frequently and with impunity.

According to Coulton,[12] while Archbishop Langton had a deacon burned for having apostatized and married a Jewess, there is no record of reprisals for the few earlier apostasies to Judaism, there being a record of two Cistercian monks having been converted to Judaism. Maitland, in a later study (Roman Canon Law in the Church of England, 1898), points to the punishment of the deacon at Oxford as indicating a change in the position of the Jews, since in the 12th Century several instances of such proselytism had occurred in England, and no punishment had followed the "crime." [13]

It would seem then, looking at this event in Oxford in the year 1222, that what happened there was not divinely ordained from the beginning of time. "Everyone" would not agree that this self-made Jew must be burnt—which would have made it the most popular verdict in the history of the universe. Nor was his death demanded by all laws, human and divine. We must look to the decrees of Innocent III which laid down the principle that all Jews were doomed to perpetual servitude because they had crucified Jesus, and also which imposed on their clothing a perpetual badge of infamy. We must also look to the special character of Archbishop Langton who was particularly zealous in his enforcement of all of Pope Innocent III's principles.

To revert to Maitland's *crie de coeur,* "whether there was anything reprehensible in putting to death this degraded clerk," well—yes. While the deacon may have "piled sin on sin" his "crime" was not enormous. It was no crime. According to William of Malmesbury, in his history of Rufus' reign, some Jews endeavored to prevail on some converted Jews to return to Judaism. They entered into controversy with bishops because the king had said that if they mastered the Christians in open argument, he would become one of their sect. There was apparently much more give-and-take in this era than Maitland was willing to recognize. What Maitland did was bring to Medieval Catholic England his own sense of Victorian values.

As Coulton observes: "There is no greater delusion than to represent the Middle Ages as a time in which everybody knew the clear bounds of self and community, of church and state." [14]

II

One may ask, without the slightest assurance of an answer: How is it that a historian, so learned and brilliant in the full grasp of his materials, falls prey to the most elementary errors when dealing with a subject that relates to him emotionally? For it is no light matter to bring acrimony to the writings of a profound, beloved jurist blessed with a style that might be the envy of any Nobel laureate

6

for literature. See for example the introduction by Helen M. Cam to *Selected Historical Essays of F.W. Maitland:*

"When Maitland died, fifty years ago, one friend noted 'the smallness of the ripple on the general consciousness caused by the passing of England's greatest historian since Gibbon and Macaulay'—and the University of Oxford sent a special message of condolence on his loss to the University of Cambridge—a gesture, as far as I know, without parallel. The union of grace, wit and humor with the most exacting sense of language is not so common that we can afford to forget Maitland." [15]

Perhaps some partial explanation may emerge by putting the *Essay,* published in 1886, in its contemporary setting.

The relative thaw against Jews in Eastern Europe under Alexander II came to an end with his assassination and the press hinted at a "secret Jewish conspiracy." In the spring and summer of 1881 a series of pogroms "spontaneously" exploded throughout southern Russia and the Ukraine while the police remained inactive. On August 22, 1881, Alexander III issued a paralyzing network of legal restrictions against Jews that was not lifted for thirty-five years. On May 3, 1882, the Central Committee passed what became known as the May laws. Russian inhabitants of villages were given the right to expel anyone as they saw fit. The great population of Jews were forced out of rural areas and congested the cities. The May laws established a strict *Numerus Clausus.* Many thousands were forced to travel abroad for their education.

In 1879 Treitschke published the first of his anti-semitic articles. In 1881 Eugen Duhring wrote a book, *The Jewish Question as Racial, Ethical and Cultural Problems,* in which he suggested "remedies" which Hitler was later to apply. In 1881 a mass petition drafted by Bernhard Forster, Nietzsche's brother-in-law, signed by a quarter of a million citizens, demanded the social segregation, the economic boycott, and the removal from public life of all Jews. Treitschke called anti-semitism brutal and hateful, but a "natural reaction of the German folk-sentiment against an alien element which has occupied too large a space in our life." [16] He demanded the complete assimilation of the German Jews and a stoppage of Jewish immigration from the eastern borderlands of Germany. His prominent position as a national scholar and popular prophet gave to anti-Semitism in Germany a recognized standing, perhaps even more than Richard Wagner's racial Jew-baiting. Treitschke's motto, "The Jews are our misfortune," served as a rallying banner for the German anti-semitic movement of the next sixty years.[17]

In England Baron Lionel de Rothschild took the oath of office that allowed him his seat as the first Jewish member of Parliament, in 1858. In 1870 The University Test Act removed the difficulties in the way of a Jew becoming a scholar or fellow at an English university. Till then fellows had to be ordained in the Church of England. When in 1881 the outburst of violence in Russia brought the position of the Russian Jews prominently before the world, it was their co-religionists in England who took the lead in organizing measures for their relief. The immigrants being excluded from most of the cities of the continent, the burden of receiving most of the Russian refugees moving westward fell on England and protests began to be heard against the "alien immigrants." [18]

Toward the end of his brilliant career, Maitland turned his talent to bring to the attention of the English-speaking world the work of Otto Gierke, the German legal historian and philosopher. He translated a small part of Gierke's book to which he gave the title, *Political Theories of the Middle Age*,[19] and to which he contributed a valuable introduction. Now Gierke is a source which is seldom mentioned, even among the experts. There is no current encyclopedia that carries his biography. It may be well worth our while to see what "diseases" he spread and what, if any, Maitland contracted.

Jerome Hall asks an interesting question in this regard: "Is 'historical jurisprudence' correctly classified as 'legal philosophy'? We know what is meant by Legal History—we think of Maitland and Holdsworth in that connection. Similarly the idea of a history of legal philosophy is not difficult to comprehend—e.g., Pound and Bryce.

"But what is historical *jurisprudence,* i.e., historical legal philosophy? The ambiguity of joining terms like 'historical' and 'philosophy' in the above manner is apparent. For the one, in its traditional sense, deals with unique, non-repetitive events whereas the other is a generalization par excellence." [20]

According to Ernest Barker,[21] the beginnings of the School of Historical Law in Germany are rooted, in their immediate origins, in a reaction against Natural Law—a reaction against its rationalism, against its universalism, and against its individualism. Instead of pure *ratio,* covering the world and time with its system of rational rules, and proceeding from and returning upon the individual, there was to be substituted the *Volkgeist,* immersed in the historical flood of its own particular development, and immersing the individual in the movement of its own collective life. Law, on this view, is essentially *Volksrecht:* it is the product, in each nation, of the national genius. A new movement of thought thus returned to the idea of national law, which Rome had slowly transcended in the millennium of legal development which lay between the Twelve Tables of 450 B.C. and the issue of the Digest in A.D. 533. It rejected as an incubus upon the growing life of nations the conception of a supernational rule of right, whether that conception took the form of adhesion to Roman law as a *ratio scripta* for all humanity, or issued in the proclamation of a new Natural Law based on pure *ratio naturalis.* The Nation revolted against Natura. This was the essence of the revolution in German thought which began a century and a half ago.

It was a revolution which was contemporary with, and largely influenced by, the French Revolution. The French Revolution, it is true, was in some respects fundamentally different. It was a revolution not against "Nature," but in the name of "Nature," it proclaimed the natural and imprescriptible rights of men and citizens, as recited in the Declaration of 1789, against an outmoded absolutism and an outworn social system. But the Revolution also proclaimed the rights of the Nation and the principle of *souveraineté nationale;* and its future course—whether, by edicts of fraternity, it sought to elicit national movements in its own support, or whether, by the oppression of its tutelage and its exactions, it involuntarily produced national movements directed against itself—was destined to encourage the philosophy of the *Volk.* It was amid the storm and thunder of the Revolution and the Empire, and, in particular, amid the passionate fervors of the movement of Liberation which followed on the battle of Jena that the theory of the *Volkgeist* and of *Volkrecht* attained its splendor.

But the Romantic movement, from which the revolution in German thought takes its beginnings, is even earlier than the French Revolution. It is a movement which we may trace as early as 1770. It is a movement back to the Middle Ages; back again, behind them, to the primeval sources of Teutonic antiquity; back, in a word, to the homely and indigenous core of the life of the German people. It is a literary movement; but it is a literary movement with an imminent philosophy of its own. That philosophy is a philosophy of the Folk, as a Being which creates language for its utterance; which utters itself through its language in folk-songs and folk-tales; and which sets the folk-songs it has written to the folk-tunes it has composed. Herder first expressed this general philosophy, from 1784 onwards, in his *Ideen zur Geschichte der Philosophie der Menschheit*,[22] a work which Gierke repeatedly cites in his footnotes, and to which, in a lecture delivered before the University of Berlin in 1903, he ascribes a large creative influence in producing the School of Historical Law.

In 1812 the brothers Jacob and William Grimm published the first volume of their *Marchen*, fairy-tales, as we now say, but the word "folk-tale" would be nearer to the purpose of the compilers. Jacob Grimm studied language in the four volumes of his German Grammar, seeking to relate its growth to the development of the people's voice and the evolution of the people's thought. He traced folk poetry in law; and he sought to recover the legal antiquities and to collect the ancient "dooms" of primitive Germany. In his *German Mythology* he recreated the ancient gods, and revealed the old figures of Folk-religion and popular superstition. In his hands the Folk became no longer an abstraction, or a postulate of theory, but a storied and documented being, expressed in language and ballad and saga, in legal *Weistumer* (instruction) and religious myths.

The conception of the folk-soul not only inspired the philologist and student of literature. It also inspired the historian; and we may trace its efforts in Niebuhr's *Roman History*. Above all, it also inspired the philosopher. We may say of Hegel and the Hegelians that they took the Folk and lifted it into the heavens of metaphysics. In their philosophy the Folk becomes a Mind, and not only a Mind, but also an incarnation of the Eternal Mind. In its eternal process, the Eternal Mind incorporates itself in folk-minds, which are the incarnations of God in time and space, and indeed *are* God, as He operates within the limits of Here and Now. They are therefore divine; and because they are divine they cover every range of life, and they are also final and right, within their space and time, for all that they cover. Organized in the State, which is the highest power of its life, the Folk attains the highest synthesis of all its faculties.[23] The State reconciles the private "Morality" of its individual with the formal system of "Law" which has been developed on the plane, and to meet the needs, of a common "economic society," and it reconciles them both in the higher unity of a system of social ethics, or *Sittlichkeit,* which is the final reach of the mind of the Folk, strung tense by the power of the State—a reach that carries it back "into the life of the universal substance."

The great tide of Romantic thought (which has flowed in Germany ever since, now deep and now diminished) flowed also over the field of law. Indeed it appeared in law even earlier than in philosophy. Hegel's *Philosophy of Law and Outlines of the State* was published in 1821; but the foundations of the School of Historical Law, which regarded law as the historic product of the folk-mind (with the jurist in some way collaborating in the process of production) go back to the eighteenth century. Mention has already been made of the influence of Herder's *Ideen*[24] of the years 1784-5; and Justus Moser, lawyer and statesman, who published his *Patriotic Phantasies* between 1774 and 1776, may also be counted among the forerunners. Hugo, Professor of Law at Gottingen, was already teaching, about 1789, that "the law of a people could only be understood through the national life itself, since it was itself a part and expression of that life." But the definite appearance of the School of Historical Law may be dated from the foundation of the University of Berlin in 1809. The foundation of the University was itself the expression of a national movement: It had been preceded by Fichte's *Reden an die deutsche Nation*[25]; it counted among its earliest professors Fichte himself, the historian Niebuhr, and two great jurists—Eichhorn the Germanist, and Savigny the Romanist. It was these two (both young men) who wedded law to history, under the common auspices of the Folk which lives in time and speaks in law. They founded in collaboration a journal of historical jurisprudence; and they devoted long and laborious lives to the historical study of law.

Savigny argued, "For law, as for language, there is no movement of cessation. It is subject to the same movement and development as every other expression of the life of the people . . . All law was originally formed by custom and popular feeling, next by jurisprudence—that is by silently operating forces." In the strength of this view he protested against codification, which would imprison the development of law in an iron cage; he protested against *Naturrecht* and all its works; he sought to secure free course for the flood of a people's thought, flowing "with pomp of waters unwithstood." It is in this succession that Gierke, though he does far more justice than Savigny to the idea of Natural Law, essentially and fundamentally stands. Has he not said, *ex cathedra,* that "in any scheme of thought which proceeds on the premise that the social life of man is the life of super-individual entities, the introduction of the Volkgeist into the theory of law will always continue to be regarded as the starting-point of a deeper and profounder theory of society"?

"We have to remember Gierke's fundamental belief in the reality of the Group-person. On this basis the State becomes a real person; but so also do those groups in the State which are more than mere partnerships or simple collections of individual persons; and so, again, does the Church, as a group which stands side by side with the State. One real Group-person may somehow be greater and more authoritative than another; but so far as they are all 'real,' they all seem to be on a level. It is hardly clear how Gierke really conceives the relation of State and Society. But on

the whole he seems to regard the State as a force control-
ling and regulating society and its various groups; and he is
anxious that it should do its shaping liberally, recognising,
in its regulation of groups, that it is regulating 'real
persons.' "[26]

Maitland reports in a summary of Gierke's position: "A
universitas (or corporate body) . . . is a living organism and
a real person, with body and members and a will of its
own. Itself can will, itself can act . . . it is a group-person,
and its will is a group-will." [27]

According to Harry Elmer Barnes the founder of this
position was the German jurist Johannes Althusius (1557-
1638).[28] "His theory of the state as a hierarchy of constitu-
ent groups was broadened out by his modern interpreter
Otto Gierke, in his *Genossenschaftslehre,* which was spon-
sored and clarified by the eminent English historian and
jurist, F. W. Maitland. Briefly, the doctrine is that the state
is not a collection of individuals, but an aggregation of
groups. These groups, in turn, are not merely a plural number of individuals, but an organization of individuals de-
signed to achieve a definite purpose. As purposive groups
they are psychic organisms, possessing not a fictitious but a
real psychic personality." [29]

III

We must ask what is at stake here. Is there a digression
from the Deacon's Apostasy at Common Law to the *Genossenschaftslehre* of Otto Gierke? Let us examine the "Natural Law" from which the Germanists were rebelling.

Cicero declares that "Law is the highest reason implanted
in Nature which commands what ought to be done and
forbids the opposite." [30]

Aquinas, seeking to combine Greek and Old Testament
notions, says, "The light of Thy countenance, O Lord, is

signed upon us [Ps iv 7]," thus implying that the light of natural reason, whereby we discover what is good and what is evil, which is the function of the natural law, is nothing else than an imprint on us of the Divine light. "It is therefore evident that the natural law is nothing else than the rational creature's participation of the eternal law." [31]

"A law that is not just, seems to be no law at all. Wherefore such laws do not bind in conscience, except perhaps in order to avoid scandal or disturbance, for which cause a man should even yield his right according to Matthew v 40,41: If a man take away thy coat, let go thy cloak also unto him." [32]

The school of natural law met with great success, particularly since it affected the political philosophy of the eighteenth century, Locke most profoundly but also Montesquieu. The reaction came to be organized in Germany as well as France. In the United States its most conspicuous opponent was Oliver Wendell Holmes:

"The question remains as to the *Ought* of natural law. . . . But for legal purposes a right is only the hypostasis of a prophecy . . . A dog will fight for his bone. The most fundamental of the supposed preexisting rights . . . the right to life . . . is sacrificed without a scruple not only in war but whenever the interest of society . . . is thought to demand it." [33]

In contrast we may quote Justice Field: " [The 14th Amendment] was intended to give practical effect to the 1776 declaration of inalienable rights, rights which are the gift of the Creator." "As in our intercourse with our fellowmen certain principles of morality are assumed to exist—and that among these are life, liberty and the pursuit of happiness, and to secure these—not grant them but secure them—governments are instituted among men, deriving their just powers from the consent of the governed." [34]

Morris Raphael Cohen states plainly enough: "I have

been for more than a quarter of a century advocating an avowedly normative jurisprudence as the application of judgments of value or social ethics to legal institutions; and I have not been afraid to call it a return to natural law." [35]

In 1887 Ferdinand Tonnies, a German sociologist, published a book of *Community and Society (Gemeinschaft and Gessellschaft)*, fundamental to German political thought. *Community (Gemeinschaft)* saw totality and wholeness in the group of which the individual was only part. It was formed by unconscious factors, by the deep, dark forces of instinct. It was irrational in its origins and in its ties, deeply embedded in the forces of nature, growing organically. It was characteristic of primitive and, to a lesser extent, feudal times. *Society (Gesellschaft)* was a characteristic of modern bourgeois civilization. It saw wholeness and totality in the individual, who was prior to the group owing its origin to national motives and individual interests. German social science contrasted the "organic depth" of "community," regarded as peculiarly German, with the "mechanic superficiality of society," regarded as characteristic of Western bourgeois society. The contrast was expressed as that between *Kulture* and civilization. One could then dare to doubt the value of civilization and of civilized life at all, and oppose to it the primeval forces of nature.

The revaluation of all values was undertaken by Friedrich Nietzsche. The ethics which guided Western thought and life from the time of the Hebrew prophets and Greek philosophers he rejected contemptuously as a Jewish-Christian invention for the protection of the weak and the dispossession of the strong. He wished to destroy all the accepted ethical values because, like the whole of western civilization, they were no longer able to sustain man.

For the new man he wrote new tables of law which would enable the new man to master life and direct history in the world-wide decision he felt impending. Nietzsche found nowhere as willing an audience as in the German youth who delighted in the contempt for Western bourgeois civilization.[36]

In the nineteenth century historical consciousness came fully into its own and became the dominant trait of the period. The Germans developed it into a philosophy of its own, a *Weltanschauung*. *Weltanschauung* is no rational concept. It is an intuitive contemplation of the whole. It cannot be understood by rational thinking; it is a product of the deepest instincts, not of the individual but of the collectivity. It led in Hegel and his disciple Marx to a metaphysicization of history. According to this theory, the historical process itself is a revelation of the divine; the divine is no longer the law and limit of everything historical, but is identical with history. Everything now becomes historically necessary. In 1933 the German philosopher Martin Heidegger greeted the Nazi totalitarian state as historically inevitable and stressed that the philosopher must therefore avoid moral indignation.

The late eighteenth century was marked by pronouncements of human equality, but inequality was no less demonstrable or relevant. As premises for social theory they bore identical status. One can emphasize physical differences and illogically deduce intellectual and cultural inequalities. In France the right attacked rationality, universality, democracy and worked out a position of great coherence and force. This includes the rights of man, popular sovereignty and the social contract which is responsible for all the troubles which have assailed France since 1789 and the defeat at the hands of Prussia.

Among the most passionate critics of the Enlightenment and the Revolution was Gobineau, who introduced the pernicious brand of political thinking known as Racism, the central element to the holocaust committed by Nazi Germany.

17

"I will not discuss the moral and intellectual worth of individuals taken one by one." [37] Such an anti-individualist approach considers morality and intellect not as personal matters but within the context of race alone, establishing a hierarchy of group typologies within each of which the myriad human variations are annihilated. Such a race theory, closely assimilable to Gierke's Group Personality, is morally totalitarian, leading to the annihilation of all other value systems. There is a justification by blood which removes man beyond the conventional ideas of good and evil.

With the premise of equal human rights and dignity once denied, that of racial inequality once accepted, a perilous journey begins that will not be easy to halt. For racism is too much a matter of Absolutes. It must pose directly the uncompromising question as to who shall be killer and who victim—the ultimate political question.

Finally Maitland is to be judged as a legal historian. Helen M. Cam notes the difficulty. "If we attempt to define the peculiar merits of Maitland as a historian we shall find that there is one and the same explanation for his special gifts and for his failure to attract the general public. Law was his guiding light; and the legal approach to history is too impersonal for the average reader, who demands incident and characterization from his historical writers." [38]

In spite of their genius and originality, it was a pity that such English historians as Maitland and Toynbee should fall under the Teutonic spell with its naive espousal of periodic crises and impending doom. While western society has engaged in unprecedented growth and prosperity since the seventeenth century, Germany remained on the fringe and never fully accepted enlightenment or emancipation. An impartial view of this era is certainly not one of decline but of considerable attainment and the promise of more to come. A new age of scientific achievement buttressed with the reality of liberty and tolerance has come into being. A great extension of personal liberty under the impartial protection of law is taking place. The very violent resistance of Russia and its allies gives testimony to the strength of the Western movement.

In flat contradiction to the "theory of decline" the modern west is strongest and most successful. The contradictions it endures are more the growing pains of youth than symptoms of senility. But German thought rejected the civil society of England and America and the Declaration of the Rights of Man and proclaimed the innate superiority of "indigenous" German thought.

Despite the popularity of Goethe and Kant, anti-Western attitudes predominated. Politically the center of German intellectual life shifted from Western Germany, which had once been part of the Roman Empire, to the east that the Germans had conquered from the Slavs in the Middle Ages. There the great military power of Prussia brought into being the idolization of the State, the embodiment of reason and ethics. In the German Romantic movement the individual became a law unto himself and his desires self-validating. The State was understood as an organic individual of a higher kind endowed with unique character and rights.

Werner Sombert: "The German heroic concept lays emphasis on duty; it looks on the state not as a contrivance for securing happiness, but as an organism, a spiritual whole." [39]

The military defeat of 1918 brought Germany to nihilism, breaking absolutely with western civilization and seeking childish security in the blood and soil of dogmatic faith.

Notes to The Deacon and the Jewess

1. Frederic William Maitland, *The Deacon and the Jewess; Or, Apostasy at Common Law. Landmarks of Law,* Ray D. Henson, ed. (Boston: Beacon Press, 1963), p. 249. Originally published 2 Law Quarterly Review 153 (1886).

2. Ibid. p. 251. But this council seems to have exceeded the bounds of the Fourth Lateran Council which after all affirmed the *Constitutio pro Judaeis.* This papal constitution, first formulated by Nicholas II in 1061 and renewed by numerous medieval popes, provided a broad charter of Jewish liberties. See Edward H. Flannery, *The Anguish of the Jews* (New York: The Macmillan Co., 1965), p. 101. The unique and most extraordinary measures taken by the Council was the prescription of a distinctive dress for Jews and Saracens. (At a later date, heretics, prostitutes and lepers were included.)

The English bishops at Oxford in 1222 issued an injunction forbidding Christians, under pain of excommunication, to sell any provisions to the Jews. Malcom Hay, *Thy Brother's Blood* (New York: Hart Publishing

Co. 1975), p. 90. But the king refused to sanction such a barbarous proposal. The king, Henry III, was a child of five and the orders were decreed through the regent Hubert de Burgh.

3. Ibid., 257.
4. Ibid., 258.
5. Ibid., 253.
6. Hannah Arendt, "Antisemitism" (New York: Harcourt, Brace & World, 1951), Preface p. x.
7. Henson, op. cit. p. 249.
8. Ibid.
9. Frederick Pollock and Frederic W. Maitland, *The History of English Law* (London: Cambridge University Press, 1968), Vol. I p. 114.
10. Ibid., Vol. II, p. 550.
11. B. Blumenkranz, *The Dark Ages,* Cecil Roth, ed. (Israel: Rutgers University Press, 1966), p. 84.
12. G.G. Coulton, *Medieval Panorama* (New York: Meridian Books, 1955), p. 352.
13. This point is made by Joseph Jacobs in *The Jewish Encyclopedia,* Vol. V, p. 164. I have examined the book referred to pp. 158-179, which seems merely to be a slight expansion of *The Deacon and the Jewess.* The copy I read, however, is kept in the rare book collection of the Columbia Law School library and the conditions attached to its consultation were not such as to induce scholarly serenity. As I was also suffering from the effects of a surgical procedure, I decided to let the point made by Jacobs stand, subject to correction.
14. G.G. Coulton, *Medieval Village, Manor, and Monastery* (New York: Harper & Brothers, 1960), p. 62.
15. *Selected Historical Essays of F.W. Maitland,* ed. Helen M. Cam (Boston: Beacon Press, 1962), p. ix.
16. Hans Kohn, "Prophets and Peoples" (London: Collier-Macmillan, Ltd., 1961), p. 116.
17. Ibid.

18. See *The Letters of Frederic William Maitland,* ed. C.H.S. Fifoot (London: Cambridge University Press, 1965), letters # 158, 159, 163, 164; but *cf.* letters 215, 216, 218, 222 to Charles Gross, American Jewish professor of history at Harvard with whom he had a most affable and fruitful relationship.

19. (London: Cambridge University Press, 1900). Reprinted (Boston: Beacon Press, 1958).

20. Jerome Hall, *Readings in Jurisprudence* (Indianapolis: The Bobbs-Merrill Company, 1938), p. 121, n. 3.

21. See Otto Gierke, *Natural Law and the Theory of Society,* trans. with an introduction by Ernest Barker Vols. I & II (London: Cambridge University Press, 1934. Reprinted Boston: Beacon Press, 1960), p. L.

22. Johann Gottfried von Herder, *Reflections on the Philosophy of the History of Mankind,* abridged with an introduction by Frank E. Mannel (Chicago: The University of Chicago Press, 1968).

23. For more recent analyses of the "Volk" in German consciousness see, e.g., Hans Kohn, *The Mind of Germany* (New York: Harper & Row, 1960; George L. Mosse, *The Crisis of German Ideology* (New York: Grosset & Dunlap, 1964; and Norman Cohn, *Warrant for Genocide* (New York: Harper & Row, 1966), Ch. VIII.

24. Herder, op. cit.

25. Johann Gottlieb Fichte, *Addresses to the German Nation,* ed. George A. Kelly (New York: Harper & Row, 1968).

26. Ernest Barker, op. cit., p. xxiv.

27. F. W. Maitland, *Political Theories of the Middle Ages,* p. xvi.

28. See *The Politics of Johannes Althusius,* tr. and abridged by Frederick S. Carney (London: Eyre & Spottiswoode, 1964).

29. Harry Elmer Barnes, *Sociology and Political Theory*, (New York: A.A. Knopf, 1924), pp. 29-30. For what seems to be the logical extension of the Althusius-Gierke thesis see Nietzsche, *Beyond Good and Evil*, tr. Walter Kaufmann (New York: Vintage Books, 1966), p. 203.—"Life itself is *essentially* appropriation, injury, overpowering of what is alien and weaker ... Even the body within which individuals treat each other as equals ... if it is a living and not a dying body, has to do to other bodies what the individuals within it refrain from doing to each other: it will have to be an incarnate will to power, it will strive to grow, spread, seize, become predominant ... because it is *living* and because life simply *is* will to power."

30. Hall, op. cit., p. 19.

31. Ibid., p. 29.

32. Ibid., p. 39.

33. Ibid., p. 260.

34. Ibid., p. 294.

35. Morris Raphael Cohen, *Reason and Law* (New York: Collier Books, 1961), p. 171.

36. Hans Kohn, *Political Ideologies of the Twentieth Century*, 3rd Ed. Rev. (New York: Harper & Row, 1966), Ch. VI.

37. *Gobineau: Selected Political Writings* ed. Michael D. Bidiss (London: Jonathan Cape, 1970), p. 26.

38. Helen M. Cam, op. cit., Introduction p. IX.

39. Hans Kohn, op. cit., p. 258.

The Stained Glass Window

Edmund Burke, in his speech to the House of Commons March 22, 1775 on Conciliation with the American Colonies, observed: "I do not know the method of drawing up an indictment against a whole people."

This, Sir, is the method. It should never be forgotten that what is involved is a capital charge against a whole people from which derives logically capital punishment.

Chateaubriand (1768-1848) in his sermon for Good Friday: "The people had cried out . . . His blood be upon us and upon our children . . . God listened to this vow of the Jews and answered their prayer." [1]

Bossuet (1627-1704): "O cursed race! Your prayer will be answered only too effectively; that blood will pursue you even unto your remotest descendants, until the Lord, weary at last of vengeance, will be mindful, at the end of time, of your miserable remnant."[2]

Jules Isaac remarks: "It is not a historic theme but a stained glass window picture." [3] Robert Graves and Joshua Podro give us some idea of the nature of that "stained glass window picture":

"After much patient research and experimentation, the

Dean of York and Mr. O. Lazenby, a foreman glazier, have at last successfully restored the fourteenth-century 'Jesse' window in the nave of York Minster. This originally showed a vine with curved branches and twisted tendrils, Jesse lying at the foot, kings and queens standing within the trunk, prophets posted in the whorls, and a majestic crowned Virgin dominating the scene. In 1789, one William Peckitt, who was commissioned to repair the window, replaced Jesse with an erect king of his own creation, giving him a grotesque eighteenth century head and a dress made from a fifteenth century canopy enclosed in the frame of David's harp. He also removed the labels from the twelve prophets, distributed their shoes and fragments of the Virgin's crown in odd corners of the window, set a queen's head on Daniel's shoulders, jumbled the vine's branches, and placed the Virgin's hand, with half the book she was holding, on the ground at Samuel's feet. The window is now once more in something like its original condition, though several heads, broken or lost in Commonwealth days, have had to be replaced by later ones." [4]

Why is the allusion to "a stained glass window picture" so appropriate? "There was of late some sentiment to grant unapprehended Nazi murderers of Jews the protection of a twenty-year statute of limitations. But nineteen hundred years are evidently not long enough when the 'guilt' of 'unbelievers' is at stake as a dogma. A technique dear to ideology is to make time stand still. The question of 'the Jews' and the Crucifixion must be posed because it has become an obsession within the Christian soul. . . . A theology that consents to verbalize respecting 'Jewish responsibility for the Crucifixion' is not theology at all, or, if that word must be used, it is devilish theology. Any theology that flouts justice and the time process, contradicting not alone the higher reaches of goodness but even the limited goodness of ordinary jurisprudence, is the enemy of truth." [5]

The blink of an eye is as a millennium to an anti-semite.

"In the irrationality, fury, and terrible persistence of anti-semitism we appear to be confronted with a form of social perversity that simply has no equal. Different racial conflicts have their day, but hatred of 'the Jews' possesses an incomparable duration and a unique intensity. It is the one chronic disease of Western culture." [6]

A few months after the preliminary vote of Vatican II declaring that "what happened to Christ in his passion can in no way be attributed to the whole of the Jewish people living at that time much less to those living now" for Christ underwent his passion and death freely, because of the sins of all men and out of his infinite love, the saintly Pope Paul VI, who failed to extend diplomatic recognition of the Vatican to Israel (in contrast to its recognition of Arab countries), said during a Lenten mass that the gospel reading for that Sunday "is a grave and sad page. It describes, in fact, the clash between Jesus and the Jewish people. That people, predestined to receive the Messiah, who awaited him for thousands of years and was completely absorbed in this hope and in this certainty, at the right moment, where, that is, Christ came, spoke and presented himself, not only did not recognize Him, but fought Him, slandered and injured Him, and in the end killed Him." [7]

Yet was not the New Testament community, a community of Jews, persuaded that Jesus of Nazareth was the Savior of *Israel?* To pretend otherwise is ridiculous. As a missionary of the Christian gospel, Paul, erstwhile Pharisee of the Pharisees, stood in the synagogue of Pisidian Antioch to attest that God has "brought Israel a savior, Jesus," from the posterity of David (Acts 13:23).[8]

We do not appear to realize—perhaps we do not wish to know—that until the church admits unqualifiedly, and goes out of its way to proclaim to the world the anti-semitic proclivities within sections of its basic canon, hostility to Jews will not be finally rooted out anywhere in Christian teaching.[9]

Christianity has not taught that there are bad Jews along with bad Huns, Vandals, Arabs, Indians or Japanese; instead it has taught that "the Jews" killed God. To *be* a Jew is to deserve punishment—Jews are hated without limitation of date or boundaries of place.[10]

So here we have to deal with a mystery, with a reconstruction of a stained glass picture window, not perhaps in the relaxed style of Conan Doyle or Agatha Christie. We are working against real time in the real universe when we deal with a capital charge. Prejudice grows into conviction, conviction into action, and the hangman is always accommodating.[11] The charge of deicide has been brought against the Jewish people.

Whether we can uncover "layers" of accretion and arrive at a pure bedrock of historical accuracy is doubtful. As A. Powell Davies points out,[12] historical and theological scholars have known for a long time that the traditional view of Christian origins is not supported by history so much as by theology. Scholars have long been aware of the impossibility of knowing where Jesus was born or by what means the portrait of him in the first three Gospels can be reconciled with the quite different portrait of him in the Gospel of John. During the first centuries of its development in the Mediterranean area, the debt of Christianity to Paganism was extensive. There are also important resemblances between the Essenic organization and the early Christian church.

Christianity is not the teachings of Jesus and his disciples but the Greek salvation cults of the Pagan Mediterranean. The Apostle Paul saw that Appolos, Mithras and Osiris could be made to bow before his own Hebraic Adonai and their saviorhoods and blood redemption could be absorbed into the Messiah of Israel to become the world-Christ.[13] Christ was elected the Savior God by majority vote at the Council of Nicea, 325 A.D.

The Gospels do not reproduce historical truth; they are

apologies conditioned by and dependent on their time. Without directly suppressing them, the authors were able to retain old sources by putting them into new contexts. Naturally enough, this technique of placing sentences in altered contexts gave rise to a series of insoluble contradictions. They did not write history; they invented it.[14] History is always written by the victor. But what a victor! The Romans claimed a human defeat over the Jews. The Christian claim was total. It proclaimed the defeat of Judaism in art, religion, literature, music, and philosophy. For almost two thousand years, the Jewish community was largely compelled to live among people who were convinced that Jewish defeat and degradation had far deeper significance than mere human rejection. Wherever Jews went in the Christian world, they were met by peoples convinced that they were the rejected of God.[15]

"In view of the enormous use made by the early Gentile Christians of their Jewish heritage, the Septuagint and the works of Philo, the Jewish liturgy and the whole Graeco-Jewish religious vocabulary which the church took over, it is strange that the Christian attitude toward Judaism was not more sympathetic. But dogmas are harder to get around than facts. And the anti-Jewish dogma was deeply fixed in Christian thought and devotion. 'His blood be on us and on our children' (Matt. 27:25), 'Your father the devil' (John 8:44)—these dreadful utterances, which ought to find no place in any sacred book, stand out conspicuously in the New Testament. They are the flaming posters put up by the world-wide anti-Jewish propaganda of the early Christians and their pagan neighbors. This terrible inheritance of hatred and bigotry the early church passed on to the medieval, and the medieval to the Reformation and post-Reformation churches. Peter 'the Venerable,' the ninth abbot of Cluny (1092-1156), addressing the Jews on the futility of their religion, and avowing that he intended to benefit their souls—'if you *have* souls'—this is only one of the more despicable of Christian examples of medieval anti-Judaism. The whole ghastly story of fanatical hatred, tension, rioting, pillage, and murder which continued for centuries, especially in the Rhineland and Low Countries during the Crusades and after, is not often told in histories of the church, but the record is not complete without it. From this accumulation of prejudice and fanaticism the Reformation might have been expected to set European society free. But not so. The theological basis of the Reformation was Paulinism, chiefly as understood by Luther and Calvin, not the teaching of the Gospels, which were demonstrably Jewish in tone and outlook as well as in language and presuppositions. The result was a total identification of Judaism with 'self-righteousness,' reliance for salvation on 'works of the Law' and 'confidence in the flesh.' That Germany, the home of the Reformation, was a refuge for Jews during two centuries does not disprove the patent fact that basically the Protestant dogmas were anti-Jewish, nor that Luther's own personal influence was anti-Jewish. At long last, the rising tide of modern 'anti-Semitism' got under way in Germany soon after the Franco-Prussian War in 1870, chiefly in army circles." [16]

"The Christian New Testament is interpreted from a purely dogmatic point of view: 'the gospel' is not the teaching of Jesus, but the interpretation of Jesus, chiefly his death and resurrection, as set forth by Paul. Thus prejudice always rebounds upon those who share it. Our own sacred book is distorted, and our own religious life deformed, in the interest of maintaining a theological principle, namely, the 'rejection' of the Jews and the divine condemnation of 'moralism' and 'legalism'!" [17]

God has endowed man with the faculty of sight but has included a defect known as a "blind spot" where the fibres of the optic nerve join the retina of each eye. The "Shma," the basic affirmation of the Jewish faith, begins with the word "Hear." John Dewey distrusted philosophy based upon visual evidence and habitually used the verb "grasp." To "grasp" an idea was to encounter it from various angles and subject it to verification on more than one plane.[18]

"Blind Spots" are unfortunately not confined to minute retinal blockage but extend to the great mental areas of conceptual blanks and blunders.

"Millar Burrows, who is no ordinary scholar, but a distinguished Semitic specialist who has worked on the Scrolls almost from the beginning, tells us that 'After studying the Dead Sea Scrolls for seven years, I do not find my understanding of the New Testament substantially affected. Its Jewish background is clearer and better understood, but its meaning has neither been changed nor significantly clarified.' And he goes on to say that perhaps he 'simply cannot see what is before his eyes.' 'When visiting archeological excavations,' he interestingly informs us, he has sometimes been 'unable, with the utmost good will, to see things pointed out by the excavators.' Scholars, being human, sometimes fail to distinguish between trained perception and uncritical imagination." [19]

The message seems plain. It is difficult to overcome a vision of belief when confronted with evidence to the contrary. The profession of theology is not particularly concerned with evidence in the legal or even the historic or scientific sense although while the prejudice is operative it will affect the person holding it no less than the one against whom the prejudice is directed. To call for the correction of certain teachings is not to substitute a new set of dogmas for the old, but rather a process that seeks to find out what evidence will support one belief instead of its alternative.

In light of these considerations we may now study some writings in the New Testament which are most cited to sustain the charge of deicide brought against a whole people.

Mat. 26:47: Judas came, one of the twelve, and with him a great crowd with swords and clubs, from the chief priests and the elders.

Mat. 26:57: Then those who had seized Jesus led him to Caiphas the high priest, where the scribes and the elders had gathered.

Caiphas—a certain confusion surrounds the issue of identity. No name is given to the High Priest in Mark or Luke. In Luke and John the name is Annas. In John, Caiphas is interpolated as being the son-in-law of Annas. In John 18: 19-33 Annas is the officiating high priest who interrogates Jesus.[20] It is not unfair to imply that it was scarcely possible for the role of the high priest to have been as prominent a factor in the proceedings against Jesus as the Evangelists' account would indicate. Nor could their uncertainty be due to the lack of prominence of the high priest since according to Josephus he had held this office for eighteen years.[21] At the outset we are confronted with a suspicion of fundamental unreality.

Mat. 26:59: Now the chief priests and the whole council sought false testimony against Jesus, that they might put him to death, 60: but they found none, though many false witnesses came forward.

We may pause here to comprehend the scene. Now if the "whole council" implies the Sanhedrin, it could not possibly be a true reference for the Sanhedrin was forbidden to hold council on a festival or the eve of a festival. No sessions of the Great Sanhedrin might take place on the Sabbath, Feasts or the days preceding, nor did they ever meet at night. But Jesus was tried on the night before the Passover which, that year, fell on a Sabbath.[22]

Romans did not interfere with the administration of Jewish religious laws. The Sanhedrin even had authority to execute Romans found guilty of entering a part of the Temple reserved for Jews alone. A Roman soldier who desecrated a Torah was executed.[23] In other words, Romans recognized the Jewish right to pass the sentence of death on offenders against the Mosaic law and to execute them. The account in John 19:7: "We have a law, and by that law he ought to die, because he has made himself the Son of God" becomes inexplicable because the crime of blasphemy was punishable by death by stoning (Acts 7:58). The Great Sanhedrin, had its procedure been followed, could have condemned Jesus to death, without referring the case to Pilate, if his offense had been a religious one. But political offenses lay outside its jurisdiction.

Had the issue proceeded judicially, Jesus would have been tried by the Great Sanhedrin, after the Passover, on a charge of interfering with the Temple administration, the maximum penalty being thirty-nine stripes, but most probably to be released with a warning.

Pontius Pilate used special courts of inquiry which would include the collaborationist Chief Rulers to investigate political disorders not provided for by the Mosaic law and to recommend a fitting disposition.[24] Except by courtesy of the procurator, these special courts had no standing. But the Chief Priest's special court was not one that Jesus could recognize as being competent to judge him.

According to Mark 14:62 and Mat. 26:64, Jesus uttered no blasphemy. Blasphemy consisted in taking the name of God in vain (Ex. 15:7 and Leviticus 24:10-16). The Pharisees held that it was not punishable by law unless God had been cursed in his own name which implied the pronunciation of the tetragrammaton. Jesus had used the phrase "the right hand of *Power*" and thus did not blaspheme. "Hellenistic Judaism—though prepared to expect a celestial quality in the Messiah, still thought of him as rising out of humanity. Historical doubt has therefore been raised

32

whether Jesus ever actually described himself as God, for in his language it meant claiming to be JHWH, an impossible claim for any devout Jew, to whom JHWH was unique and utterly other-than-man, the distinct partner in a personal encounter and contract, with a proper name never reducible to adjective. The Jewish faith had stressed the non-humanity of God and the non-divinity of man." [25]

"Blasphemy" therefore should read "treason," namely rebellion against Rome. "Ironic though it be, the most certain thing known about Jesus of Nazareth is that he was crucified by the Romans as a rebel against their government in Judaea. The fact is recorded in the four Christian Gospels, and the execution, on the order of Pontius Pilate, is mentioned by the Roman historian Tacitus, writing early in the second century. The Christian attestation is particularly significant. That the founder of their faith had been put to death on a charge of sedition could hardly have been invented by Christians; for such a fact obviously caused the Roman authorities to view the faith with suspicion, as Tacitus' statement shows. The early Christians had, indeed, a strong motive for suppressing so embarrassing a fact; that they did not do so surely attests both its authenticity and notoriety." [26] This agrees with Luke xxii:70 where the court declares that Jesus had claimed to be "son of God," that is to say King; and with John xi:48 where the charge is one of endangering the national security.

Yet the utterance of "treason" against Rome was not an occasion for Caiphas to rend his garments, unless it was the certainty of the knowledge he had of the brutal and contemptuous treatment Rome had in store for its traitors and thus was done in anticipation of the death of Jesus.

According to John there is no meeting of the Sanhedrin by day or night, rather an interrogation by Annas, who sends Jesus to his son-in-law Caiphas, who sends him to Pilate. There is no hint of a Jewish trial of Jesus in the

Gospel of John. Our minds and emotions are so stirred by the Synoptics that we almost fail to recollect that this scene is a complete blank in the Fourth Gospel. It does not exist for him. It never happened. Neither Luke nor John makes the slightest allusion to a Jewish sentence condemning Jesus to death.[27]

In Origen's refutation (186-254) *Against Celsus* 2:27 ". . . certain of the Christian Believers, like persons who in a fit of drunkenness lay violent hands upon themselves, have corrupted the Gospel from its original integrity to a three-fold and a four-fold, and many fold degrees, and have remodelled it so that they might be able to answer objections." Celsus was not alone. Contemporary with him, Irenaeus, Tertullian and Dionysius of Corinth recognized that "the writings of the lord had been unscrupulously falsified." [28]

After the Jewish rebellion 66-70, it was a great advantage to court the good will of the Roman authorities. Thus the Gospel accounts can be regarded as prosecution evidence and they are the only evidence available. It was necessary to explain the Scandal of the Cross (Gal. 5:11—Jerusalem Bible), the ignominious and uncontestably Roman punishment. Jesus was tried by a Roman tribunal, found guilty of a Roman crime and put to death by Roman soldiers and Roman means.

Eager to court Rome, the compilers patently applied themselves to presenting a version of the Passion such that Roman authority, represented by Pilate, would emerge from the affair with almost clean hands; while a responsibility so freely accepted by the Jews: "His blood be on us and on our children," would crush the Jews. The fact remains that Jesus was executed as a rebel against Rome, and not as a heretic against Judaism.[29]

The accusations of the witnesses ignored by Caiphas refer not to the "I" reported by John, but to "God" who will rebuild the Temple in three days, after Hosea 6:1: "Come, let us return to the Lord; for he has torn, that he may heal us; he has stricken, and he will bind us up. 2. After two days he will revive us; on the third day he will raise us up, that we may live before him." [30]

On the momentous scandal of "Deicide" Jules Isaac asks,[31] "At what moment did the defamatory epithet appear, the brilliant find—itself murderous—which would be made into an indelible brand, generating frenzies and crimes (homicide, genocide)?" Malcolm Hay[32] gives the honors to St. John Chrysostom (398) described by Cardinal Newman as "A bright, cheerful, gentle soul." (Are there really two histories in the universe like the two points of an ellipse which are farthest apart and yet constitute its indissoluble unity?) Surely a great deal more than this must be admitted. "The violence of the language used by St. John Chrysostom has never been exceeded by any preacher whose sermons have been recorded. These homilies have been transmitted for many generations and were used in schools and seminaries as their model where priests were taught to hate. He was the first Christian preacher to apply the word 'deicide' to the Jewish nation. It helped strengthen the tradition of hate handed on through the Dark Ages and welcomed by medieval Christendom, a tradition which has disfigured the whole history of Western Europe." [33]

Jules Isaac places the event much earlier: "The contents of the Gospels, begun in the mid-first century, carry visible marks of these polemics; this is particularly true of . . . Matthew and John . . . owing to the obvious eagerness it exhibits to slide the whole weight of responsibility for the Crucifixion from Roman on to Jewish shoulders." [34]

The great third century theologian Origen, battling with the pagan Celsus, was still taking the trouble to mention Pilate while declaring that Jesus' condemnation was above all the act of the Jewish authorities. "The Jewish nation has been condemned by God—for they crucified him (Jesus)." [35]

In *Jesus and Israel* Jules Isaac devotes an entire section of his book, pages 233-382, to examining the question of the accusation of deicide against the Jewish people. One of the principle ingredients of the Christian dogma had been voiced by St. Bernard of Clairvaux. "The Jews are for us the living words of Scripture, for they remind us always of what our Lord suffered. They are dispersed all over the world so that by expiating their crime they may be everywhere the living witnesses of our redemption." [36]

Or see a history text of more recent date (1947) for use in Catholic primary schools: "The punishment of the deicide (God-murdering) Jews was not long in coming. Thirty-six years after the Savior's death, the Roman Emperor Titus seized Jerusalem and completely destroyed the Temple. The Jews dispersed throughout the world, have never again been able to form a nation. They have wandered everywhere, considered a cursed race, an object of contempt to other peoples." [37]

Pope John XXIII at the dramatic Vatican Council II made it clear that in his view the Jewish people live at the very root of Christian salvation. He supported a brief forthright text abrogating the ancient Christian charge of "deicide" against the Jews. The draft subsequently prepared by Augustin Cardinal Bea was withdrawn under pressure from the Vatican Secretariat of State and from bishops in Arab countries. Arab diplomats declared that the new declaration fostered propaganda for the State of Israel. The council of the Greek Orthodox community in Damascus condemned the decision to declare the Jews innocent of the blood of Christ, because it is contrary to the sacred Scriptures in which Christians have always believed. "It is dogma of the church that the guilt of the crucifixion of Christ must fall upon the Jewish people until the end of the world." [38]

In direct opposition to the wording overwhelmingly approved in 1964, Pope Paul intervened in the final session in behalf of excising the "deicide" reference. The New York Times reported that the excision was a response to the claim of some that the church would be implying that it no longer believed in the divinity of Christ. As a substitute for the approved draft a statement was put forth that "the Jews should not be presented as rejected by God or accursed, as if this followed from the Holy Scriptures." And allusion is made to "Jewish authorities" who with their followers pressed for Jesus' death.

Søren Kierkegaard, who has become an icon of existential philosophic and religious thought, makes his contribution thus: "Then tell the child what befell Him (Jesus) in life, how one of the few that was close to Him betrayed Him, then the other few denied Him and all the rest scoffed at and derided Him until at last they nailed Him to the cross . . . requiring that His blood might be upon them and their children. . . . What effect do you think this narrative will make upon the child? The child would have decided that when he grew up he would slay all those ungodly men who had dealt thus with the loving One." [39]

It is difficult to believe that men so skilled and learned, when faced with the choice between objective historical investigation and literal claims of the Gospels, would choose the latter standard over the first. Ideology, which is impervious to modification, transcends the idea and evidence of alternative explanations.

" 'His blood be on us, and on our children.' Few of the sayings of the Gospels have done more harm than these, and yet they are only the invention of the redactor!" [40] There can be little doubt that the tradition has read back into the contemporaries of Jesus the hostility felt by the early Christian communities towards the Jewish Rabbis who were the most formidable opponents of their mission. We must take into account the angle of vision of a group of

Evangelists reporting an event of real contemporary conflict as having taken place during Jesus' lifetime. There was no religious difference between Jesus and the Pharisees, let alone evidence of mortal conflict;[41] the truth remains that the historical structure of Christianity is erected upon a Big Lie: *the Jews'* rejection and murder of Jesus Christ.[42]

The State of Israel and the New Testament

"The 'dialogue' could remain more or less a joke so long as the Christian side had all the advantages of power. Fortunately, Jews have equalized the situation, with their bare hands. Even those Jews who physically remain in *Galuth,* in dispersion, are free now: through Israel they are blessed with an experiential, living cause that stands in judgment upon, and vanquishes, all the immoralities of Christendom. By virtue of Eretz Yisrael, aided by a burgeoning religious and social pluralism that is post-Christian, Jews can for the first time in Western history tell the Christians to take all their anti-Semitism along to perdition with them." [43]

"In Christianity, the reason for Israel's expulsion was both the crucifixion and the rejection of Jesus, and the penalty was everlasting exile. Out of this grew an imposing theological system which identified the Jewish people with Cain. And like Cain, the Jewish people was under the peculiar care of God, who would permit this oppression, but not total destruction. From this grew the many myths of the Wandering Jew. Church theology and Christian folklore are quite explicit about this. They stress the endlessness of the exile, and the proof in the exile of the wickedness of the people who are living witnesses—in their abject lot—to the true faith of Christianity. Documentation of this is profuse."

"Now, however, history has intervened to demolish these

myths and premises wherever they may still be cherished. The full impact of this veritable earthquake in the world's attitude toward the Jew will not be felt for a long time. But the full effect of religious anti-Semitism, beginning with the Church Councils in the Fourth Century, also required generations to impose themselves on the mind and history of Europe."

"What concerns us here, however, is that the myth of a deicide doomed to perpetual exile has been repudiated by history." [44]

"It is clear that the Western Jew is no longer in Galut. He abides in diaspora by an act of the will which prior to 1947 he could not. We can accept or reject it and act upon this choice." [45]

"The concept of diaspora can be transformed for the first time in 2000 years. It need no longer represent repression and exile imposed by the restraints of a hostile world. The creation of Israel has annihilated the principle of duress in the Western world and replaced it with a community which chooses its own form of existence." [46]

"The Jewish people have a duty to survive. The faith of the Jewish people is the most authentic test yet devised of the world's integrity. The truth of every cause is validated or found fraudulent in the way in which it confronts the Jewish people. . . . What other people, destroyed and exiled for almost two thousand years, has ever been reborn? The wise men who measure the life and death of every civilization, who predict the decline and fall of every living society—what do they have to say about Israel? To have crawled out of the sewers of Warsaw, the barracks of Auschwitz, the forests of Poland, and to give birth to a people again is a marvel that no deterministic interpretation of history, no economic dialectics can possibly cope with. *This* is the moment from which Jewish theology and a theology of consolation for men everywhere arises. And this is the saving event which rescues the Jewish people from ultimate terror and despair."

"The event rescues all men: the capacity of a people to face the demonic in man and to overwhelm its own fate is a vindication not only of this people, Israel, but of the spirit of man, flickering desperately in the dark night of human anguish. Because of Israel, Jews in the Diaspora-exile may stand erect—and so may every man." [47]

Dr. Otto Frank, father of Anne, said: "The State of Israel teaches that there will be no more Anne Franks. There will be dead heroes, if need be, but no more martyrs."[48]

The historic Christian stand respecting Jews has been that they should convert or leave or die. Although Muslims today appear to have little desire for the conversion of Jews, a certain related demand is nevertheless present: the conversion to statelessness. The Jews are to accept politicide as their proper destiny. And they can leave "our land," or stay to fight and die.

Volte Face

Mat. 27:25: And *all* the people answered—

There is an irreconcilable disagreement on the time sequence of the Passion, whose pace supposedly was singularly rapid according to Mark 15:25, since ". . . it was the third hour (nine o'clock in the morning) when they crucified him." Less rapid in John 19:14: ". . . it was about the sixth hour (noon) when the sentencing occurred." Certainly a very limited time in which to involve the whole Jewish nation in the irreconcilable curse thundering through all time and space. (If Jesus followed the Essenian calendar, the course of his trial and Passion would be spread over three days rather than a few hours.) [49]

Mat. 21:8-11 (Arrival at Jerusalem): Most of the crowd spread their garments on the road—And the crowds that went before him and that followed him shouted, "Hosanna to the Son of David . . ." And when he entered Jerusalem, all the city was stirred, saying, "Who is this?" And the crowds said, "This is the prophet Jesus from Nazareth of Galilee." (See Mk 11:9-11; Lk 19:36-38.)

Mat. 21:14-15: And the blind and the lame came to him in the Temple, and he healed them . . . the chief priests and the scribes saw the wonderful things that he did, and the children crying out in the Temple, "Hosanna to the Son of David!"

Mat. 21:45-6: But when they (the Chief Priests and the Pharisees) tried to arrest him, they feared the multitudes, because they held him to be a prophet. (See Mk 12:12; Lk 20:19.)

Mat. 26:3-5: Then the chief priests and the elders . . . took counsel together in order to arrest Jesus by stealth and kill him. But they said: "Not during the feast, lest there be a tumult among the people."

Throughout Luke we hear of crowds and multitudes besieging Jesus wherever he went. Lk 12:1; 14:25; 15:1; 19:3.

Lk. 19:47-48: The chief priests and the scribes and the principal men of the people sought to destroy him; but they did not find anything they could do, for all the people hung upon His words.

Lk. 21:38: And early in the morning all the people came to him in the temple to hear him.

Lk. 22:2,6: And the chief priests and the scribes were seeking how to put him to death, for they feared the people . . . (Judas) sought an opportunity to betray Him to them in the absence of the multitude.

The evidence provided by the Gospels leaves no doubt on the point of the popularity and favorable reception of Jesus. Only Nazareth remained incredulous and stirred up against Jesus. Everywhere else the crowd was won over in Judea and Galilee. They hurried after Jesus to the shore of the lake; before the house he entered they "hung upon his words" (Lk. 19:48), staying with him three days without eating.

Mk. 14:1-2: And the chief priests and the scribes were seeking how to arrest him by stealth, and kill him; for they said, "Not during the feast, lest there be a tumult of the people." This last remark reveals the doubtful nature of Mark's later picture of their influence over the crowd in the Barabbas episode.

Even the doctrinal bias of the Fourth Gospel is confirmatory 12:19 (Jesus' arrival at Jerusalem): The Pharisees then said to one another, "You see that you can do nothing; look the world has gone after him." Also 12:42: Nevertheless many even of the authorities believed in him.

But was ever such an "about-face," *volte-face*, ever achieved in the history of mankind in a few desperate hours? Some commissioners, collaborating with and responsible only to the Roman occupying forces, have been identified in the process of securing and approving proceedings against Jesus.[50]

The dominant influence of the council was the high priest, oligarchic, subject to Rome and detested by the people. The Jewish nation could by no stretch of the imagination be identified with this caste in any way. The Evangelists themselves testify that the leaders acted unbeknownst to the people, despite them and in fear of them.

The event took place on Nisan 15 according to the Synoptics, the first day of Passover; a Sabbath or Nisan 14 according to the Fourth Gospel, the eve of Passover; neither date possible under Jewish law for such procedures. No Jews were about when Jesus was tried on the day of Passover, the most solemn feast day in the year. Jews were otherwise occupied than making a dangerous and utterly pointless show of themselves, while these Jewish chief priests and elders were at the Temple assisting at the morning sacrifice.

Was there a radical shift of opinion from one day to the next, from the arrest of Jesus to his appearance before Pilate, during which the admiration and love expressed by the multitudes changed to a murderous frenzy collaborating with their detested pagan conquerors in slaying a rabbi in Jerusalem?

The new Church lost no time in attributing to Jesus a divine nature. His death became a deicide and this abomination was destined for the Jews who had denied him. For Christianity to proceed it was necessary that the Jews be a criminally guilty people, the nucleus of Christian anti-Semitism. From the third century on, Origen formulated the problem:

"We may thus assert in utter confidence that the Jews will not return to their earlier situation for they have committed the most abominable of crimes in forming this conspiracy against the Savior of the human race. . . . Hence the city where Jesus suffered was necessarily destroyed, the Jewish nation was driven from its country, and another people was called by God to the blessed election." [51]

Mark 8:34: "If any man would come after me, let him take up his cross and follow me." This reference to crucifixion anticipates a Roman death. To anticipate the responsibility of the Jewish leaders for the death of Jesus would suggest he would have to be executed according to Jewish law. The author of Mark took every precaution that his readers should understand that it was the Jewish leaders who engineered the crucifixion of Jesus by the Romans.

Charles Guignebert concludes: "This trial (Sanhedrin) appears to be merely an artifice, clumsily introduced in order to shift the principal responsibility for Jesus' execution onto the Jews." [52] It does not seem rash to suppose that the earliest Christian records attributed all the responsibility for the death of Jesus to the Roman procurator.[53]

The probable and decisive accusation is given in Luke 23:5: "He stirreth up the people, teaching throughout all Jewry, beginning from Galilee to this place."

"The rest of the Marcan account is intended to give us the impression that Pilate was favorably disposed towards Jesus and only yielded to the implacable animosity of the Jews; but this is not historically true. The probability is that the Nazarene was arrested by the Roman police, judged and condemned by the Roman procurator Pilate or someone else." [54]

"When the Jewish people as a whole proved irreducible, it became necessary, imperatively necessary for the edification of the faithful, that the Jewish people as a whole prove evil, fundamentally evil, unworthy, laden with crimes, opprobrium, and maledictions. And when this became necessary, this became true, with a theological truth which infinitely outdistanced historic truth . . ." [55]

It was not until 1965 that Vatican II in effect repudiated the Gospel words "all the people" in these words: ". . . what happened in His passion cannot be blamed upon all the Jews then living, without distinction (nor upon the Jews of today)."

"Destroy this temple, and in three days . . ." Jn. 2:19

The author of Mark gives no explanation for the fact that in his narrative the Jewish authorities handed Jesus over to Pilate charged with sedition. A Jewish account would scarcely have been apologetic for the fact that Jesus had been put to death by the Romans. From the Jewish point of view Jesus had died an honorable death. Such a death would have been a martyrdom such as achieved by Akiba in a later period or Judas of Galilee at an earlier period, all tortured to death for their ancestral faith.

The moment in Jerusalem was one of crisis as Mark informs us that there had been an insurrection in which the rebels caused casualties, perhaps among the Roman garrison (15:7). Pilate was thus prepared for the accusation which was brought against Jesus. The first question put to Jesus by Pilate was: "Are you the King of the Jews?" (15:2.) Mark's task being to represent the death of Jesus as essentially due to Jewish malice, it must be explained how it was that Jesus was executed by the Romans as a revolutionary. His modus operandi is to show that Pilate, having recognized the innocence of Jesus, wished to set him free, but was prevented by the Jewish leaders from carrying out his judgment of clemency and forced to order the execution. Whether this Pontius Pilate was a person likely to submit to the Jewish leaders so tamely we shall shortly consider. But how is it that Pilate did sentence Jesus?

One accused of threatening to destroy the Temple and handed over as a Messianic pretender would expect short shrift from the procurator. Mark himself presents the evidence of the triumphal entry of Jesus into Jerusalem, his attack on the Temple, the insurrection and the armed resistance in Gethsemane.

Jesus is represented as foretelling the destruction of the Temple (Mk. 13:1-2). In the next chapter those who accuse Jesus of threatening to destroy the Temple are described as bearing false witness against him (Mk. 14:56-9). The denial that Jesus had spoken against the Temple is repeated later (Mk. 15:29).

The rejection of the charge, in the account of the Sanhedrin trial as "false witness," is not clear. Why does Mark represent the testimony as false? It may be that at the period of its composition, primitive Christianity continued the observance of Temple worship.

In any case the tradition at the period of the trial means that the Judges must have rejected the charge that Jesus condemned or threatened to destroy the "house of God."

Since Mark records the dismissal of the charge about destroying the Temple as false witness, why does he also represent Jesus as foretelling the destruction of the Temple—certainly a threat or a hostile attitude seemingly to contradict the representation of the charge at the trial as false. He is careful not to suggest that Jesus himself would destroy the Temple despite his prophecy. Both the Gospel of John and Acts attest the prophecy that Jesus would destroy the Temple (John 2:18-19; Acts 6:14), indicating that the charge brought against him at the Sanhedrin trial was not entirely "false witness."

These passages create an impression of artifice in composition. The Roman victory over insurgent Judaea (71 A.D.) made prominent the fact that Christian faith stemmed from the Jewish people, and that the founder of their faith had been executed, a few years before, by a Roman procurator of Judaea as a rebel against the Roman government of that country. Mark was profoundly concerned with the problem raised by the crucifixion of Jesus. At the time of his execution there were many claimants to the title of the Messiah who would deliver Israel from the hands of the hated Romans.[56]

If then Jesus had been executed as a rebel, how could this death be interpreted as a divine act of salvation? The explanation of Pilate's condemnation of Jesus, whom the author of Mark presents as a revolutionary, was to be followed by all subsequent Evangelical writings. The responsibility for the execution of Jesus lay with the Jewish authorities who forced a reluctant and wavering Pilate to their will. That such an explanation on the face of it is incredible does nothing to lessen its force.

The indisputable fact is that Jesus was put to death by the Romans, and by crucifixion as guilty of sedition against their government.[57] Consequently, if it is true that Jesus had originally been arrested at the orders of the high priest and had been condemned for his claims and actions in terms of his Temple prophecy or blasphemy, there must have been some reason for his subsequent condemnation as a rebel against Rome and his execution by the Romans. But Mark does not supply this reason.

Without explanation the Jewish authorities delivered Jesus, bound, the next morning to Pontius Pilate. In this process we can infer they must have preferred a charge of sedition because Pilate immediately asks him "Are you the King of the Jews?" (15:2). The implications of being regarded as a claimant to that title in Roman Judaea was tantamount to sedition.[58] Mark offers no explanation of the charge of sedition.

Pilate would, on receipt of this charge, proceed in an orderly and intelligible way to determine whether this charge could be substantiated and thus constitute a threat to the stability of the Roman rule, which it was his duty, with the cooperation of the native leaders, to maintain. But the underlying and stunningly successful effort of the editor of Mark is apologetical, namely to show that Jesus, the pacifist, had fully and wholeheartedly endorsed the occupying Roman government of Judaea.

Now Barabbas. . . Jn. (18:40)

Mark produced the longest running hit show in all history. The indictment of a whole people was necessary to bring forth Jesus Christ, the universal savior. This is no question of literary skill, or even religious inspiration. It is an event in which the corner of the universe was turned and the course of history altered as surely as the creation of the cosmos or the eruption of the sun. The author recast the universe in his own mould—an inconceivable achievement fully deserving the term "miraculous." Historical investigation and logic pale before this achievement. It cannot be

47

undone. It is certainly worthwhile to examine some of its elements and see how it combines into a blazing whole.

The episode of Barabbas remains a crux for New Testament scholars on historical grounds. We have no other evidence besides the Gospels for this astonishing custom.[59] Josephus, zealous in his attention to recording all privileges that Rome accorded to the Jewish people, strangely fails to make mention of so notable a grant. There is never an instance cited of the release of a prisoner on such grounds.

Its lack of logic is equally baffling in context of such notable administrators of law as were the Romans. Such a concession by an occupying force would surely disrupt orderly and effective government, particularly in an area on the edge of revolt. It would have required Pilate to release a popular leader who had just been involved in a revolt against the Roman army. What explanation could there be for such conduct by any military ruler?

Nevertheless the story was eagerly embraced for it provided great relief for the embarrassing information that the founder of their faith had been executed as a Jewish revolutionary.

Mark skillfully introduces a private note of doubt in Pilate's question to Jesus: "Have you no answer to make? See how many charges they bring against you." But Jesus made no further answer, so that Pilate wondered (15:4-5).

After this elusive suggestion that Pilate was unaware that Jesus was not guilty of the charges against him Mark continues with his improbable brief (15:6). "Now at the feast [Passover?] he used to release for them [the use of the tense indicating that this was a custom peculiar to Pilate] one prisoner for whom they asked." The statement is extraordinarily vague but it does well as prologue for the scene that is mounting.

"And among the rebels in prison who had committed murder in the *insurrection*" (15:7). There is nothing vague about this—there are rebels against Rome who are in Pilate's charge and his duty is to execute them with the ferocious and savage contempt that all Romans had for any form of treason, the *crimen laesae maiestatis.* Not only are they rebels, they are rebels who have commited murder, a charge requiring execution regardless of circumstances, but these rebels had further committed murder in an armed insurrection. There is no organized society in history that would not have executed such charges out of hand.

". . . There was a man called Barabbas." Up to now we have been dealing with the principals, the chief priests, the high priest, Peter, and Pilate. The time was early: "And as soon as it was morning" (Mk. 15-1); "When morning came (Mt. 27:1); "Then they led Jesus from the house of Caiphas to the praetorium. It was early" (Jn. 18:28). It is important to note that the Jewish people play no role and have no place in the first phase of the Roman trial. Luke alone mentions the presence of "the multitudes." It was Passover, the sabbath—the religious duties of the Jew were particular and rigorous at the Temple and at home.

But the hand of a great dramatist appears, dimming the achievements of Aeschylus, Sophocles, Euripides and their successors, and the impossible not only became visibly true but a matter of faith.

Pilate's increasingly favorable impression of Jesus is interrupted suddenly by a crowd. Here the genius of Mark transfers us from praetorium to proscenium and a scene is created that forever explains away Pilate's responsibility for the crucifixion and fixes that responsibility forever on the Jewish people.

The Romans would not have permitted a mob scene of that sort here before the very seat of Pontius Pilate, the sacrosanct representative of the majesty and power of *Senatus Populusque Romanus* (The Roman Senate and People) and the *sedia curulis* (the magistrate's chair).

When Jesus was removed from the dungeon where he had lain since his arrest, he faced a full court consisting of the presiding officer, assessors, clerks, councilors, advocates, attendants, military guards, torturers, as well as Roman citizens, *amicus curiae*—friends of the court—all of whom were required. No Roman court would have tolerated a mob to interrupt a solemn trial of treason involving life and death as well as the majesty and power of Roman law, venerated in the ancient world. Moreover no Jew would have set foot in the praetorium for they would have defiled themselves by entering the pagan judgment hall.

"And the crowd came up and began to ask Pilate to do as he was wont to do for them" (Mk. 15:7-8). At this point there is no longer the slightest pretense of history, logic or even time sequence. The design is concerned entirely to present a scene which would disguise and effectively remove Pilate's responsibility for the crucifixion. Assuming even that Pilate used to have that strange privilege, the "crowd" merely puts forth a general petition of sorts—an unspecified demand for a prisoner's release.

The procurator, in the midst of his interrogation of Jesus, instead of considering the matter in light of the tense situation in Jerusalem and consulting with his entourage, directs his next remarks to the suddenly assembled mob, who, the day before, were greeting the triumphal entrance of Jesus with loud Hosannahs and expressions of love and admiration. In direct instantaneous response to the mob's unspecified demand for *a* prisoner's release, (presumably anyone *would* suffice), he offers to continue the form of this custom of the "festival" by responding with a strikingly specific public offer. He offers to release unto them Jesus whom he calls "the King of the Jews." Had this offer been accepted, it would undoubtedly have been the signal for a general insurrection. But for Mark's purpose, Pilate's motive is made perfectly plain to his readers, "For he perceived that it was

out of envy that the chief priests had delivered him up."
(15:10). Notice that Mark's account goes beyond the formal
legalities of a Roman trial at law or any pretense of history
or common sense in that Pilate privately recognizes the innocence of Jesus; on the other hand he skillfully takes care
that Pilate does not publicly recognize this "innocence."
This would have signalled an abdication of his powers and
the supine surrender of the majesty of the Roman law to a
formless, non-descript mob. It would have further indicated
his hypocrisy in making the offer to release the "King of
the Jews" and fixed the responsibility for the crucifixion
where it belonged, on the specific orders of Pilate.

Mark proceeds in two steps. First he has made clear the
murderous intent of the chief priests. Then he relates how
Pilate's plan to save Jesus was frustrated. The unspecified
demand of the crowd for a prisoner's release is now made
specific. "But the chief priests stirred up the crowd to have
him release for them Barabbas instead" (15:11).

"We can only wonder at the speed and efficiency with
which these priestly aristocrats acted on the spur of the
moment thus to influence the crowd to demand the death
of Jesus, when that crowd had so enthusiastically supported
him against themselves only a few days before"[60] and had
come into existence moments ago with a wave of a wand.

But this is high drama and the author is not concerned
with the implications of his account of Pilate's behavior in
all this. Pilate, backed as he is in full panoply with the
powers and majesty of the law, the army alerted for disturbances during the festival, the military guard resplendent in
gleaming helmets and bucklers, the imperial eagle shim-
mering on their formidable spears, having the power and
authority to dismiss the charge, custom or no custom, is
reduced to shrinking from the seat of his power; for though
being favorably disposed towards Jesus, the proceedings are
suddenly interrupted by the crowd whom the chief priests

caused to demand the release of Barabbas, and he turns not to the councilors, advocates, Roman citizens, *amicus curiae,* but helplessly asks the advice of this makeshift crowd—"Then what shall I do with this man whom you call the King of the Jews?" (15:14).

Perhaps we can take a closer look at this tragic hero who has been elevated to sainthood in the Coptic church. Josephus reports a serious clash between Pilate and the Jews over the introduction into Jerusalem of the ensigns of a Roman cohort bearing the image of the emperor (Ant. xviii 55-9; War II 169-174). The action infuriated the people and they thronged his palace to persuade him to remove the insignia. Pilate surrounded the multitude with his men but failed to intimidate them. He finally backed down and ordered the offending insignia removed. He probably yielded because he realized he was liable to be confronted with a revolt. In another case he refused to budge. He financed an aqueduct to Jerusalem with money taken from the Temple treasury. This was met with a violent reaction by the Jewish people who resented the expropriation of Temple funds for profane purposes. Pilate disguised his soldiers in civilian dress and ordered them to attack the assembled crowd. These soldiers were recruited from the Gentile cities of the province Sebaste, or Caesarea, and harbored a deep hatred for the Jews and demonstrated keen enthusiasm in executing their orders. Many of the Jewish demonstrators were killed or wounded and Pilate was master of the day (Ant. xviii, 60-2; War II 175-7).

Earlier governors had taken care when minting their coins to avoid injuring Jewish sensitivity. They avoided any symbols connected with pagan worship or idolatry. Pilate's coins were exceptional showing such pagan symbols as the *simulum or lituus,* used in Roman sacrifices. None of Pilate's harsh successors ever dared mint such coins. This evidence of Pilate's personality invalidates modern attempts to soften his image.

Another incident of shields occurred, according to Philo, when Pilate installed gold shields in Herod's palace and refused to remove them despite the outrage they provoked. All sections of the Jewish people united, including four of Herod's sons, in protesting this act. Finally the Emperor Tiberius himself intervened (Legatio ad Gaium, 299-305).

The New Testament refers to the blood of the Galileans that Pilate mingled with their sacrifices (Luke 13:1). "One must presume that clashes between the Romans and the Jewish populace frequently took place during the major festivals, since these provided a suitable opportunity for Messianic or social agitation." [61]

Pilate's barbarous suppression of a Samaritan disturbance finally led to his downfall. A large pilgrimage gathered to inspect some supposedly holy objects when Pilate put an end to the project by dispatching his soldiers to Samaria with orders to set upon the demonstrators. The Samaritan council complained to the governor of Syria who removed him from office.

What comes through the episodes related by Josephus and Philo is a picture of a brutal tyrant remarkably tough and notorious in his contempt of the Jews.

Pilate was particularly detested by the Jews. Philo, quoting from a letter of the Jewish prince Agrippa I to Caligula, describes him as "naturally inflexible and stubbornly relentless," and he accuses him of "acts of corruption, insults, rapine, outrages on the people, arrogance, repeated murders of innocent victims and constant and most galling savagery" (Legatio ad Gaium, 301). The administration of Pilate is described as a harsh and corrupt regime. We are told that Pilate was widely disliked, that he was influenced by bribery, and that he angered the Jews by his extortions and frequent executions without trial.[62]

If Jesus was as pro-Roman as Mark makes him out to be, Pilate must have realized the serious consequences of turning loose a popular revolutionary leader while at the same time condemning to death one whom he acknowledges to be innocent. This situation is belittled by those fond of quoting John (19:12) that Pilate feared that the matter would be reported to the emperor if he freed Jesus. We must ask how Pilate would have justified such conduct to his own court as well as his report to the emperor Tiberius.

The name "Barabbas" presents a further problem. Mark's "who was called Barabbas" suggests a title that should be preceded by a personal name. Note the variant reading of "Jesus Barabbas" in some manuscripts of Matt 27:16,17. It is sometimes transcribed Bar-Rabba and means "son of a rabbi" or Bar-Abba, "son of the father." Could the crowd have clamored for the release of the man who was called "Jesus, son of the Father"? There is too much anti-Jewish polemics to pierce the veil of the historic truths with regard to the account of the Passion, but the suspicion persists that in spite of the efforts of the chief priests that ghastly morning it was really Jesus for whom the anxious crowd implored pardon. Origen, surprised to read "Jesus Barabbas" in numerous manuscripts, proposed the hypothesis that a dishonest addition was involved. But the hypothesis seems groundless, and much rather applies to the suppression of the name. H.Z. Maccoby in the periodical "New Testament Studies" (Cambridge) puts forward the theory that Barabbas means "Son of God" and "Teacher," and that he was in fact identical with Jesus. It was Jesus the people were calling for.[63]

This omnipotent procurator, in the tragic mask of perplexity, asks his subjects the Jews, his creatures and collaborators, the chief priests, what he should do with the prisoner Jesus. Mk. 15:12; Mt. 27:22.

Mark informs us that an insurrection had taken place at this time. It is a remarkable coincidence that the activities of Jesus should have been regarded as subversive by both Roman and Jewish authorities. One is forced to regard his triumphal entry into Jerusalem, his attack on the Temple trading system, and the insurrection.

Pilate, who had no scruples in the wholesale massacre of Jews and Samaritans, is deeply moved with concern about a Galilean Jew suspected of messianic agitation and pleads mercy and pity for the prisoner from the crowd: "Why, what evil has he done?" Mk. 15:12; Mt. 27:22.

This Roman administrator absolves himself of complicity and responsibility by performing the symbolic Jewish ritual of washing the hands. Mt. 27:24. Origen realized that such an act was absolutely contrary to Roman procedure where the Judge assumed responsibility for his acts.

Only a supreme dramatist would interrupt a trial involving the life or death of a prisoner to allow the chief judge to leave his court chambers and assembled entourage to come to the street where a crowd has suddenly assembled. Incredibly, this iron-fisted governor, ready to repress bloodily any insurrection or even threat of insurrection, finds himself required to please a mob of idlers by consenting to free a notorious agitator imprisoned on charges of sedition and murder. The formalistic rule of Roman justice which ringed the ancient world had abdicated all the customary rules of procedure for the trial of Jesus.

Most incredible of all, "all the people," the pious, the patriotic, the idlers, the scoffers, all suddenly filled with rage against Jesus, throng at the feet of Pilate, the abhorred Roman butcher, to force his reluctant hand to take their prophet, admired and loved only a day before, and have him put on a cross by Roman soldiers according to Roman practice.

"One of two things" argues Jules Isaac: [64] either this was a random crowd, fairly small for the chief priests to have been able to work them up against Jesus in a matter of minutes; or else this was a hired mob, or the sort that is so easy to whip up in big cities. We all know how these spontaneous demonstrations work. Jesus did not die as the victim of his people. To maintain the contrary demands an inveterate, an absolute prejudice, or blind submission to a tradition—a hardy tradition, utterly poisonous, a murderous tradition—which leads to Auschwitz.

That is why the historian has the duty to state categorically:

No, you do not have the right to say, to write, to teach that "the Jewish people . . . fully assumed responsibility for the death of their Christ."

Augstein puts the metaphysical question to us: "What would have happened if Pilate and Caiaphas had flogged Jesus and let him go? Paul and the evangelists, notably John, do not let themselves get led away by the contradiction that, on the one hand, the rules of this world did not recognize the secret wisdom of God—'if they had, they would not have crucified the Lord of glory' (I Corinthians 2:8)—and that, on the other hand, they had to carry out the will of God (Caiaphas does not speak 'of his own accord' John 11:51). So men infinitely reproached for having killed Jesus, for the 'murder of God,' really had no chance not to kill him. How furious God would have been if his plan of salvation had been thwarted and Jesus had only been condemned, like Paul, to forty stripes less one." [65]

The author of Mark has been concerned to present the Jewish leaders as responsible for the death of Jesus. The Barabbas episode is masterfully utilized to explain how the intention of the Jewish leaders to destroy Jesus actually took the form of the Roman execution for sedition. The Romans used the punishment of crucifixion as a deterrent against members of a subject people who had offended against the Roman state. If Jesus died on the cross, then he died for rebellion against the Romans. But Mark's Jesus endorsed the Jewish obligation to pay tribute to Caesar.

Thus, by shifting the responsibility for the crucifixion from the Roman governor to the Jewish leaders, a most embarrassing problem for the Christians at Rome was suitably alleviated.

Through the figure of Pilate, it is demonstrated that Christianity and the state can co-exist.[66]

"And all the people answered, 'His blood be on us and on our children!' " Mat. 27:25.

With the material at hand let us see if we can perceive an arrangement of the stained glass window picture, about which, while historical verification is not possible, enough internal inconsistencies may be set aright to present the matter in a new and more logical setting.

"Now the chief priests and the whole council sought false testimony against Jesus that they might put him to death, but they found none, though many false witnesses came forward." Mat. 26:59-60.

If "the chief priests" and the "whole council" sought *false testimony* why did they not make use of the evidence provided by the many false witnesses that did come forward? Was the testimony inconsistent with verifiable fact, self-contradictory, or were the witnesses of an order of men simply not to be trusted? The epithet "false witness" is not merely a descriptive term but comes as a conclusion, a final judgment after rigorous inquiry into the legal and factual material presented as judicial evidence before the court. But *if* false testimony was sought and they had suborned persons to give false evidence about Jesus, the Jewish leaders were unaccountably punctilious in rejecting that evidence. If they had planned a rigged trial before a kangaroo court surely they would have been less scrupulous about observing the rules of evidence and the affair would have proceeded apace without knotty legal problems blocking the path.

"His blood be on us and on our children!" The language of this phrase is troublesome in more ways than one. In the first place Jewish people do not speak this way. As a matter of fact no people speak this way, calling down consequences upon the heads of their remote descendants to the end of time for which they are responsible neither morally nor factually. It is simply too fearsome a wager, beyond all bounds of reason, risk and conscience.

The certainty that the council had before them *false witnesses* indicates that these witnesses had been examined by men skilled in these matters, so they should not collapse before the tribunal and merely strengthen the case of the defendant against whom charges had been brought.

What was the method and manner of examining potential witnesses in a criminal trial before a council? Here comes to hand the Talmudic tractate "Sanhedrin" (Court), the name of a legal treatise divided into eleven chapters. It deals with the judicial powers of courts, qualifications for the office of judge, and with legal procedure in criminal law (See Jewish Encyclopedia XI, p.44 ff.). Chapter five concerns the examination of witnesses regarding the time, place, and circumstances of the case, and the credibility of the testimony given.

J. Shachter and H. Freedman in the introduction to the English translation of the Talmud note: "In the eyes of Christian students, *Sanhedrin* has always occupied a favored place among the tractates of the Talmud on account of the light which it is capable of throwing on the trial of Jesus of Nazareth." [67]

Whatever light is capable of being thrown on the trial of Jesus has been successfully sheltered under a bushel by any

Jewish or Christian Hebraist for the entire two thousand years of controversy.

"How were the witnesses inspired with awe? Witnesses in capital charges were brought in and intimidated thus: Perhaps what ye say is based only on conjecture, or hearsay, or is evidence from the mouth of another witness, or even from the mouth of a trustworthy person: Perhaps ye are unaware that ultimately we shall scrutinize your evidence by cross-examination and inquiry? Know then that capital cases are not like monetary cases. In civil suits, one can make monetary restitution and thereby effect his atonement; but in capital cases he is held responsible for his blood (sc. the accused's) and the blood of his (potential) descendants until the end of time, for thus we find in the case of Cain, who killed his brother, that it is written: The bloods of thy brother cry unto me: Not the blood of thy brother, but the Bloods of thy brother is said—i.e., his blood and the blood of his (potential) descendants." [68]

How familiar the phrases, yet how fresh the context. These are the instructions required to be given by judges in capital cases in order that they may impress upon potential witnesses the gravity of giving false evidence and thereby bringing the moral guilt of murder upon a whole world.

One must wonder how "all the people" can have been instructed in and familiar with the oral law concerning the duties of judges to be able to commit to memory the exact phrases required to be recited by a potential member of the Sanhedrin in a highly technical treatise on legal principles and procedural law. This at a period when Talmud was not as yet reduced to writing and was of necessity familiar only to that circle of students admitted to the academies conducted by the masters.[69]

The only possible place the dreadful words of Matthew 27:25, "His blood be on us and on our children!" can be logically fitted is during the examination of Jesus before Caiphas (Mt. 57,59; 'the high priest' Mk. 14:53-56; in John 18:12-19:33, it is Annas who conducts the interrogation), where, following the procedure of the Talmud, the witnesses would accordingly be solemnly warned prior to giving testimony before the assembled tribunal.

The malicious displacement of this phrase by the editors of Matthew took place between 115 and 130 A.D. when it attained its present state of corruption, most likely at the time of Bar Kochba's bloody rebellion when Christian apologists were attempting to demonstrate that they were loyal subjects of the empire, having no link with Israel.

As for Jesus' alleged blasphemy, "nothing in the Nazarene's teaching constituted formal heresy from the Jewish point of view." [70] This is demonstrated by the first Christian community composed of Jews who observed the Law strictly. They were neither accused of blasphemy nor heresy and suffered no persecution. "The members of that church saw themselves as an integral part of Israel" [71] and the evangelization of the Gentiles had no place in the policy of the original Jewish Christians. (The episode of Stephen, apparently instigated by Paul, was a conflict between Hebrews and Hellenists.) Only after the innovations of Paul were Christians regarded as heretics. The church then turned its attention to the Gentiles, attributing to Jesus a divine nature whose death became a deicide, the most abominable of sins, which could draw reproach on the head of Jews for all time. "For the organization of Christianity, it was essential that the Jews be a criminally guilty people." [72]

"In our own day, and within our own civilization, more than six million deliberate murders are the consequence of the teaching about Jews for which the Christian Church is ultimately responsible, and of an attitude to Judaism which is not only maintained by all the Christian Churches, but which has its ultimate resting place in the teaching of the New Testament itself." [73]

At the Nuremberg trials of the Nazi war criminals a German general was asked how such things could happen. He replied: "I am of the opinion that when for years, for decades, the doctrine is preached that Jews are not even human, such an outcome is inevitable." [74] Responsibility for the nearly achieved success of the German plan ought not to be restricted to Hitler and his gangsters, or to the German people. The plan nearly succeeded because it was allowed to develop without interference.[75]

The blood accusation has been answered. The stained glass window has had at least one fragment restored to the place in the jig-saw where it originally belonged. The infamy, the curse, the punishment of Israel, a punishment without appeal in perpetuity may perhaps be put aright in Christian consciousness replacing ideological phantasy with historic and spiritual reality.

"We do not appear to realize—perhaps we do not wish to know—that until the church admits unqualifiedly, and goes out of its way to proclaim to the world, the anti-Semitic proclivities within sections of its basic canon, hostility to Jews will not be finally rooted out anywhere in Christian teaching." [76]

Notes to
The Stained Glass Window

1. Chateaubriand, F. René de, cited by Malcom Hay, *Thy Brother's Blood* (New York: Hart Publishing Company, 1975), p. 327.
2. Ibid., p. 14.
3. Jules Isaac, *Jesus and Israel* (New York: Holt, Rinehart & Winston, 1971), p. 348.
4. Robert Graves and Joshua Podro, *The Nazarene Gospel Restored* (New York: Doubleday & Company, 1954), p. V.
5. A. Roy Eckardt, *Elder and Younger Brothers* (New York: Schocken Books, 1973), pp. 117, 119.
6. Ibid., p. 28.
7. Ibid., p. 125—As quoted in *The New York Times* 4/5 and 5/8, 1965.
8. Ibid., p. 138.
9. Ibid., p. 126.
10. A. Roy Eckardt, *Your People, My People* (New York: Quadrangle, 1974), p. 87.
11. See Richard L. Rubenstein, *The Religious Imagination* (Boston: Beacon Press, 1971). "The Germans taught

the world that human technology can make genocide psychologically, morally, and physically practical," p. XV. "Genocide is radically novel. The Jewish situation *has* changed radically" p. XVI.

12. A. Powell Davies, *The Meaning of the Dead Sea Scrolls* (New York: The New American Library, 1956), p. 84.

13. Ibid., p. 92.

14. Johannes Lehmann, *Rabbi J.* (New York: Stein and Day, 1971), pp. 108, 110, 111.

15. See Richard L. Rubenstein, op. cit., p. XIV.

16. Frederick C. Grant, *Ancient Judaism and the New Testament* (New York: The Macmillan Company, 1959), pp. 14,15.

17. Ibid. For a more radical view questioning the historicity of the Gospels see Rudolf Augstein, *Jesus Son of Man* (New York: Urizen Books, 1977).

18. See, e.g., Corliss Lamont, Editor, *Dialogue on John Dewey* (New York: Horizon Press, 1959), pp. 95-96.

19. A. Powell Davies, op. cit., p. 83.

20. See Jules Isaac, *The Teaching of Contempt* (New York: Holt, Rinehart and Winston, 1964), p. 133.

21. Ibid, p. 133.

22. Sanhedrin 35 a. But cf. Haim Cohn, *The Trial and Death of Jesus* (New York: Harper and Row, 1971) and references cited in A. Roy Eckhardt, *Your People, My People* op. cit., pp. 29-37.

23. Josephus Ant. XX, 117, cited by S.G.F. Brandon, *Jesus and the Zealots* (Manchester: Charles Scribner's Sons, 1967), p. 105. Ant. XX 113-7; War II 228-31 cited *The World History of the Jewish People*, Vol. VII, M. Stern, Ch. IV, p. 152.

24. Robert Graves and Joshua Podro, op. cit., p. 670. See also Hyam Maccoby, *Revolution in Judaea, Jesus, and the Jewish Heritage* (New York: Taplinger Publishing Company, 1980), p. 70 and references; pp. 154-155.

25. James Shiel, *Greek Thought and the Rise of Christianity* (New York: Barnes and Noble, Inc., 1968), pp. 46-47.
26. S.G.F. Brandon, op. cit., p. 1.
27. Jules Isaac, *Jesus and Israel,* op. cit., p. 303. Hyam Maccoby, op. cit., p. 155.
28. Ibid., pp. 293, 294.
29. S.G.F. Brandon, op. cit., p. 282. Hyam Maccoby, op. cit., p. 157 passim.
30. But cf. Brandon, op. cit., 234 ff.
31. Jules Isaac, *Jesus and Israel,* op. cit., p. 240.
32. Malcom Hay, op. cit., p. 27.
33. Ibid., p. 31.
34. Jules Isaac, op. cit., p. 240.
35. Ibid., p. 241.
36. Ibid., p. 247.
37. Ibid., p. 254.
38. A. Roy Eckardt, *Your People, My People,* op. cit., p. 43, 44.
39. Soren Kierkegaard, *Training in Christianity,* tr. by Walter Lowrie (Princeton: Princeton University Press, 1944), pp. 176, 177.
40. Charles Guignebert, *Jesus* (New York: University Books, 1956), p. 470.
41. See Paul Winter, *On the Trial of Jesus* (Berlin: Walter De Gruyter & Company, 1961), p. 133.
42. A. Roy Eckardt, *Your People, My People,* op. cit., p. 37.
43. Ibid., p. 216.
44. David Polish, *The Higher Freedom* (Chicago: Quadrangle Books, 1965), p. 23.
45. Ibid., p. 41.
46. Ibid., p. 44.
47. Alice and Roy Eckardt, *Encounter with Israel* (New York: Association Press, 1970), p. 253.
48. Ibid., p. 224.

49. See Johannes Lehmann, *Rabbi J.* (New York: Stein & Day, 1971), Ch. VII.

50. See Jules Isaac, *Jesus and Israel,* op. cit., p. 283.

51. Leon Poliakov, *The History of Anti-Semitism,* Vol. I (New York: Schocken Books, 1974), p. 23.

52. *Jesus* (New York: University Books, 1956), p. 464. For an interesting alternative see Haim Cohn, *The Trial and Death of Jesus* (N.Y.: Harper & Row, 1971), Ch. V. The Sanhedrin assembled not to try Jesus but to supersede the Roman process and save his life by persuading Jesus not to plead guilty to the charges. In the absence of acquittal, Jesus had to be persuaded that He would not again engage in treasonable activity and they would plead for a suspension of sentence.

53. Charles Guignebert, ibid., p. 465.

54. Ibid., pp. 467-468.

55. Jules Isaac, *Jesus and Israel,* op. cit., p. 239.

56. See S.G.F. Brandon, op. cit., pp. 112-113.

57. Ibid., p. 253.

58. Ibid., p. 254 (note 1).

59. Charles Guignebert, op. cit., p. 469.

60. S.G.F. Brandon, op. cit., p. 261.

61. M. Stern, *The World History of the Jewish People,* Vol. VII, Ch. III. "The Reign of Herod" (New Brunswick: Rutgers University Press, 1975), p. 130.

62. Ibid., p. 128.

63. Rudolf Augstein, *Jesus Son of Man* (New York: Urizen Books, 1977), p. 170, note. See also Hyam Maccoby, *Revolution in Judaea,* op. cit., pp. 154-155.

64. Jules Isaac, op. cit., 358.

65. Rudolf Augstein, op. cit., p. 175.

66. Ibid., p. 168.

67. *The Babylonian Talmud,* Seder Nezikin, Vol. III, *Sanhedrin,* (London: The Soncino Press, 1935), p. XII.

68. Ibid., Sanhedrin 37 a, p. 233.

69. See Howard Clark Kee, *Jesus in History* (New York: Harcourt, Brace & World, Inc., 1970), p. 162, where with unconscious knowledge the author states: "The acceptance of this responsibility is attributed by Matthew to the *Jewish leaders* [italics mine] in the dreadful words of Matthew 27:25: 'His blood be on us and on our children!' " See Morton Smith, *Clement* (Cambridge: Harvard University Press, 1973), p. 198 on Pharisaic "secrecy."
70. Leon Poliakov, op. cit., p. 18.
71. S.G.F. Brandon, op. cit., p. 168, also 122-125.
72. Leon Poliakov, op. cit., p. 21.
73. Malcom Hay, *Thy Brother's Blood*, op. cit., p. 11.
74. Ibid., p. 3.
75. Ibid., p. 4.
76. A. Roy Eckardt, *Elder and Younger Brothers*, op. cit., p. 126.

The Sermon and the Synagogue

In the fourth decade of this century, I was giving serious attention to the possibility of pacifism as an alternative to a political and military madness that seemed to be sweeping the world. It was not the Gandhian equivalent to war which pitted one temporal power against another, but rather a radical rejection of all temporal authority when it conflicted with divine authority.

The core of this thought was the Matthean account of love for one's enemies as an absolute, unshakable conviction. (Matt. 5:38.) As I discussed this point with the elders known to me, I was assured that this thought, whatever else it may be, was not Jewish. To accept that Matthean guide was to cross an unbridgeable chasm which divided Judaism from Christianity.

That this point of view is still a dominant conviction, widely held, is made evident by consulting the writings of the late Abba Hillel Silver, a reform rabbi, spiritual leader of one of the largest liberal Jewish congregations in the country.

"Judaism rejected all doctrines of nonresistance and all

forms of pacifism. . . . We do not solve the world's problems of crime and wickedness by turning the other cheek to the smiter or by giving also our cloak to him who would take our coat. . . . It is one thing to be forbearing and forgiving; it is another to submit to evil as a matter of principle, to turn the other cheek to the oppressor." [1] "The principle of self-defense in personal life as well as in national life is the same in Jewish law: 'If one comes to kill you, kill him first!' " [2]

But this thought is not confined to the rabbinate, liberal or conservative. Here, in the bright, shiny, new *Dictionary of the History of Ideas,* bristling with sophisticated ideas and original insights, we find: "Pacific themes pervade the Judaic tradition; we need only remember that the daily prayers of the Jews for more than three thousand years have concluded with a petition of peace. . . . These attitudes are continued in the early Christian rejection of the *Lex Talionis* and the replacement of negative commandments such as 'Thou shalt not kill' by the positive responsibilities of love. The classic Christian formulation is of course the Sermon on the Mount with its gentle advocacy of nonviolence, of the love of one's neighbor, of the infinite value of the soul and of humanitarian charity and benevolence." [3]

Jamnia (or Jabneh) became the seat of Jewish scholarship even before the destruction of the Temple by Vespasian. Johanan ben Zakkai asked him as a special favor to spare Jamnia and its scholars.[4] It became the religious and national center of the Jews and remained so till the time of Bar Kochba.

The author of Matthew, after the destruction of the Temple, found a rival in Johanan ben Zakkai and his followers who were writing rival accounts of historic Judaism. There is sufficient evidence to justify the claim that Jamnian Judaism was consciously confronting Christianity. It is reasonable to inquire whether Matthew was also consciously confronting Jamnian Judaism.[5]

R. Traverse Herford, a Christian Hebraist of impeccable credentials, "motivated by a deep-seated sense of justice," published a historical study, *The Pharisees.*[6] Herford is regarded by many Jewish scholars as eminently fair.

The Pharisees represented a popular movement that arose in the Third Century B.C. in reaction to the priestly class of conservative scribes who based all authority on the written law. They expanded the Torah, formulating their decisions to meet the changing and evolving needs of the common people. While the Sadducees confined their ritual to the Temple, the Pharisees inaugurated the use of the Synagogue with services and education available to all.[7] The two authorities tended to be in conflict.

Yet so fraught with misunderstanding is Herford's notions of the relationship of Jesus to the Pharisees that it would require a good-sized treatise fairly to present a documented opposition. I select one example which he regarded as presenting the crux of his position: "The only attitude of both parties throughout the short career of Jesus was that of distrust and fear on the one side and indignant denunciation on the other. . . ."[8] ". . . The details differed as between one encounter and another. But they all serve to illustrate . . . the sharpness of the conflict between Jesus and his opponents. It is not necessary . . . to deal with them all seriatim. But something must be said of the *great denunciation* [italics mine] in Matthew xxiii (cp. Luke xi, 42-54) which, whatever may be thought of it, certainly forms an essential part of the representation of Pharisaism in the New Testament. . . . Nothing can soften the hostility expressed in it; and, *whatever its origin,* it sums up and focuses in burning indignation the antagonism between the Pharisees and Jesus as felt on his side. I find no difficulty in believing that Jesus himself said what is there recorded."

This is the awesome indictment beginning with "Woe to you, scribes and Pharisees, hypocrites! . . ." One of the key points of Herford's message is the phrase, "whatever its origin." But in its origin lies the crux, the very possibility of understanding the context and essence of the "Great Denunciation." There is indeed "no difficulty in believing that Jesus himself said what is there recorded" for these are the very words used by the Pharisees in criticism of their own members, of "The Plague of Pharisees" recorded in the Talmud, Sotah 22 b.

The "hypocrite" from the Greek meant an *actor* which has no Aramaic equivalence and must be regarded a mistranslation. A feigned or painted Pharisee emphasized the outer appearance of piety without regard to pure religious motivation. The feigned Pharisees are separated into seven categories.[10]

"The whited sepulchres" of Matt. xxiii 27, far from being an adornment (i.e. a white wash), were to protect from ritual defilement people who accidentally touched them, providing a protective layer as well as making them conspicuous in darkness. Luke xi 44 omitted the phrase.

It is most likely that Jesus himself was a Pharisee. Pharisees were wrapped in the praying garment the entire day, not merely during services in the Synagogue. The fringes of his garment were touched by a woman in the street (Mk. v 27; Matt. ix 20; Lk. viii 44). "And he taught in their synagogues, being glorified by all." (Lk. iv 15.) The true Pharisee served God for His own sake without any thought of self-interest. Jesus followed this, forbidding his disciples to serve God either for fear of punishment (Matt. xxiii 23) or hope of reward (Lk. xvii 7-10).

Those who tithed mint, dill, and cummin (Matt. xxiii 23)

were "Doom-fearing Pharisees." No law compelled a farmer to tithe such self-sown herbs, but the Doom-fearers treated it as a safeguard against the torturers of Hell. This verse is an invective against the feigned Pharisees. (Also Lk. xi 37-54.)

A Pharisaic rule about the defilement of cups was that if the outside only were defiled, the inside might be considered clean, whereas if the inside were defiled, it became unclean both inside and out (Berakoth 52 a & b).

It must be a matter of concern if one's friends can write: ". . . and if the Pharisees, when Jesus died on the cross, stood by consenting to his death, though it was not of their doing, the followers of Jesus have amply, if very humanly, revenged themselves during all the centuries since. But that belongs to a later stage." [11]

The activity and achievements of Jamnia are symbolized in the character and work of Johannan ben Zakkai, 70 A.D. He was followed by Gamaliel II and the foundations had been truly laid for the triumph of Pharisaic Judaism.

Rivals to the dominant Pharisaic elements within Jewry itself had to be eliminated. Zealots were discredited and largely liquidated by the war. The Essenes were decimated but did not die out in 70 A.D. While the Pharisees admired the priesthood and mourned the loss of the Temple, there was much in the priesthood that they could not but condemn. The predominantly lay Pharisees found themselves opposed to the priesthood in fact although they accepted it in principle. It was necessary to deal with the Sadducees as the priests were sufficiently influential.

In Matthew good works demanded of Christians are described and summed up in the Golden Rule (7:12). Explicitly in the description of its blessedness (5:1-11) and implicitly in that of the demands made upon it, the Christian community is set over against Old Israel. Matthew makes clear that the Old Israel has been rejected in favor of a new community (21:33-45), the parable of the vineyard (27:15-26), where the guilt of the people of Israel as such is prominent.

Matthew places "the Jews" as a totality over and against the church and particularly isolates the Pharisees as the significant group with which he is concerned. Warning is given against the *teaching* of the Pharisees. (Luke 12:1 warns against the *hypocrisy* of the Pharisees. Mark warns of the "leaven of the Pharisees and the leaven of Herod.") Although there is a recognition of the Pharisees as sitting in Moses' seat, there is a violent denunciation of them because of their hypocrisy (Mt. 23:1-36). There is a personal animus against Pharisees. The phrase "generation of vipers" is applied to them, esp. 23:13-36. The characteristics condemned in the Pharisees are almost precisely those described in the Sermon on the Mount. The conflict between Pharisaism and the Gospel is not merely a traditional one for Matthew. It has for him a special, living Matthaean concern.

The implication of the question raised is that the Pharisaism which with Matthew was concerned was not only that which confronted his Church locally, but that wider Pharisaic movement led by the sages who sat in Moses' seat, at Jamnia. Is it likely that the developments within Pharisaism at Jamnia were known to him and affected his church? Did they work in comparative seclusion so that the Christian leaders went their way uninformed about and therefore uninfluenced by them, or was their activity of necessity widely known among Christians, as among Jews? The indications are clear that the latter was the case.

The historically significant force in first century Judaism was Pharisaic. And it was this force that the Church and especially Matthew had to oppose. The full significance of the work of the sages at Jamnia is grasped by realization of the fact that they were Pharisees bent on applying the Torah to the concrete situations of their lives. They could never have been tempted to forget that the Torah was given that men might *live* thereby. Their specific aim of providing Judaism with a new center and the measures taken to ensure it could not but have repercussions throughout Jewry and outside their ranks.

Paul Winter notes: "In the whole of the New Testament we are unable to find a single historical reliable instance of religious differences between Jesus and members of the Pharisaic guild, let alone evidence of a mortal conflict." [12]

A generation after the death of Jesus the differentiation between messianic and "normative" Pharisaism was sharpened. The Christian-Jewish sect was differentiated and separated from the moderate wing of Pharisaic Jews. Violent opposition to Pharisaism depicts a state of affairs which came about only several decades after the crucifixion. Messianists were deeply disappointed with Pharisees (Luke 19:39). Pharisees endeavored to curb messianic enthusiasm of the church which was resented in apostolic circles. As the Christian-Jewish sect differentiated themselves more sharply from the moderate wing of the Pharisaic Jews, the Apostolic Evangelists came to depict as a historical state of affairs that which had come about only several decades *after* the crucifixion. Romans judged proclamation of "another king" (Acts 17:7) disloyal to the emperor. Romans in their zeal to eradicate "pernicious superstition" (Tacitus) also persecuted Jews who had not been affected by the messianic-apocalyptic fervor.

Fault was not found with Christ himself but rather with the practices of the disciples (Mk. 2:18-23). "And some of the Pharisees in the multitude said to him, 'Teacher, rebuke your disciples' " (Luke 19:39). The conduct not of Christ but of the disciples attracted unfavorable comment. The effort of Christ was to introduce and lay down a "halakha" which would regularize the actions of the disciples and give sanction to their particularist or sectarian interpretation of the Torah. This was the vision of a group differing in interpretation of legal observances. However, the narrative of Matthew is presented as if reporting on events that took place in the lifetime of Christ. The conflict was not between Christ and his contemporaries, but a conflict between his disciples and other Jewish groups of a later age, namely the destruction of the Temple 70 A.D.

In Luke 13:31-3 the Pharisees warn Jesus against the danger which threatens him from Herod, that is, they are friendly. In Matthew this is not so. The Pharisees—who as his contemporaries were busily engaged in establishing the law in Jamnia—have become the villains of the piece. Chapter 24 is a divine Judgment on Judaism by reason of the fall of Jerusalem. The sins of Jerusalem are made vivid. Its populace appears hostile in contrast to Luke, who portrays them as sympathetic to Jesus, particularly in his hour of death. Matthew's comment on his rival contemporaries: "Your house is forsaken and desolate" (23:37 f), when it was in fact flourishing in its pristine growth.

Despite the passage of a generation after the death of Christ, when disputes between Pharisaic and Christian-Jews were activated, the violent opposition to Pharisaism depicted in Matthew is contemporary hostility retrojected into the lifetime of Christ. It is this easy transposition of events which makes Matthew so plausible and alive. This is also the editorial scheme of Mark and John.

The period when Matthew emerged was the period of the codification of the Law in Judaism and the formulation of worship. The bearing of this on the Sermon on the Mount is that it was necessary to provide a Christian counterpart to Jamnia. It was the desire to present a formulation of the way of the New Israel at a time when the rabbis were engaged in a parallel task for their community.[13]

II

With this brief introduction we may attempt to partially comprehend the most universal message of love ever given to an eager world hungering for a glimpse of the true faith.[14]

At that period of time when Jesus walked and taught at the shores of Galilee and the Mount of Olives, retaliation in case of damage to a person had been superseded by money penalties.[15] The law of talion [retaliation: eye for eye, tooth for tooth, etc. (Lev. 24:17-21; Matt. 5:38,39)] had long before been ousted. Had Jesus attacked this principle, he would have been guilty of a strange anachronism. There is in Jewish history no instance of this law ever having been carried out.

To the slogan "eye for an eye," the author of this section opposed the rule "Resist not evil." The rule is illustrated by the example in which a man had his ears boxed; in this case, the other cheek should be offered.

Let us suppose that the slogan "eye for eye" literally had meant actual talion, revenge for mutilation, and Christ had attacked this principle as being superseded. In that case the grossest of inequities follows, which would not be accepted either in civil or Rabbinic law, for the illustration he provides for the proposed new position appears excessively inept and weak, a slap in the face. Would he not have said, "Whosoever tears out one of your eyes, forgive him and do not require one of his be torn out"? In today's colloquial use of language we may say, "turn the other cheek" even for the most serious cases, but it would violate the historical

75

use of language to transport our proverbial use backward into New Testament times.

The offense of smiting a man's cheek was cited not as a proverbial case covering all kinds of injury, even the gravest, but as the best available example of a situation in which the demand of talion (eye for an eye) was *not* to apply. In the case of mutilation the law of talion as cited was neither superseded nor attacked.

In point of fact the author of this passage was not thinking of the law of mutilation at all. A slap in the face is a case not of mutilation but of insult, a very different thing. The choice of this example is evidence that what was being pronounced immoral is not the law of talion concerning mutilation, but that concerning *insult.* A man should be meek under an insult—that was his teaching—and not insist on such redress as the maxim "eye for eye" would give him, which was a sum of money for this kind of insult and such a sum for another kind. A list of fines quoted in the Talmud may be found in the tractate Baba Kamma 86a-93b governing the law of insult. The same Mishna, 83b, gives the authority that "Eye for Eye" means pecuniary compensation.

It follows then that in the mind of the author of this passage, the maxim "an eye for an eye" governed the law concerning insult which in turn was the basis for the fines to be paid by him who had committed an insult to the offended party. In the eyes of the author that maxim, far from enjoining literal talion for mutilation, simply stood for the idea of accurate reparation, the exaction of amends precisely corresponding to the wrong done. In the case of insult there had never been any talion—how could there be?—but always money penalties. The maxim "eye for eye" and its horrifying character can have reference only to fines.

Once this is recognized, three points, otherwise incompatible, become intelligible and provide strong confirmation of the interpretation submitted.

1. Both in Roman Law and in the Mishna the case of smiting a man's cheek serves to illustrate just that situation where there is insult only but no damage to the person.

2. Neither of the two further examples in Matthew ("If anyone sue and take your coat, let him have thy cloak also;" and "Who would compel you to go a mile, go with him twain") is a case of mutilation. Into no order of logic, law, or religion can such appalling *non sequiturs* be coupled. Whatever hand arranged these words in their present place did so not to combat the ancient law of retaliation in kind, but regarded the cry "An eye" etc. as characterizing him who stands on his rights and honor, what we might term a "solid citizen," instead of humbling or even humiliating himself before his fellow man. The Matthaean hand proceeded from the refined Rabbinic meaning of the "Eye" maxim as signifying the claim to accurate, wisely cultivated compensation.

3. When Christ quoted the old maxim, he significantly omitted the most important first clause of Lev. 24:17-21, "Life for life" and used only Eye and tooth. This omission must be regarded as of the utmost significance. In the case of homicide, the Rabbis did not abolish retaliation, not in theory. A murderer was liable to capital punishment save by escape into a city of refuge (Num. 35:11-12). The clause "Life for life" was not divested by the Rabbis of its literal meaning in the way "eye" and "tooth" was done. The two parts of the maxim drifted apart in law and in the minds of the people. The clause "Life for life" belonged to the realm of public criminal law, connected to the death penalty. "Eye for eye" belonged to private law, connected with money compensation, not unlike the body of modern law known as "Torts." Had "eye for eye" implied actual talion,

the omission of "Life" would be incomprehensible. The separation of the two clauses was complete and final.

The religious implication of the abolition of the ancient rule of talion to one of monetary compensaton is simply enormous. It goes far beyond the legal system of Torts which is concerned with a wrong done to you, an affront to your pride and dignity. The religious impulse is to remind the victim, the prospective plaintiff in a law suit, that the wrongdoer is your brother before God. The center of concern shifts from soothing ruffled feelings to a humility which cannot be wounded, a giving of oneself to his brother which would achieve greater and more lasting results than can be effected by the narrow victory of a legalist justice. Insult aimed at a victim's dignity as a human being, and thereby at the image of God, was regarded by the Rabbis as a terrible sin. A few examples from the Talmud follow:

"They who suffer insults but do not inflict them, who hear themselves reviled and do not answer back, who perform religious precepts from love, of such the Scripture says, 'And they that love him are like the sun when he goeth forth in his might.' " Judg. 5:31. Note the close approximation to the messages of the Sermon on the Mount, as popularly received.[16]

"It is better for a man that he should cast himself into a fiery furnace rather than that he should put his fellow to shame in public." [17]

"The striking of his fellow—or putting to shame by a hurtful remark was the typical *Rasha*—godless man." [18]

"A man should always strive to be rather of the persecuted than of the persecutors as there is none among the birds more persecuted than doves and pigeons, yet Scripture made them alone eligible for the altar." [19]

"All these fixed sums stated (for insult) specify only the payment civilly due for Degradation. For regarding the hurt done to the feelings of the Plaintiff, even if the offender should bring all the 'rams of Nebaioth' (Isa. 60:7) in the world, the offense would not be forgiven until he asks him for pardon." [20]

"Resist not the wicked man" or "Do not prosecute the wicked man" (Isa. 59:12; Jer. 14:7) would be no less in agreement with the Rabbinic attitude than "Resist not evil."

It is precisely this most direct attack on your personality which the sayings here discussed expect you to bear without resentment. It breathes the spirit of the Rabbinic teaching (Gamaliel II) at the end of the first century A.D. If you are struck you must forgive the offender even though he does not ask your forgiveness (Judah b. Ilai, mid-second century). At the conclusion of every prayer, repeated thrice daily by the observant Jew, the supplicant recites, "May my soul be silent to those who insult me, be my soul lowly to all as the dust."

In Rabbinic law the case of smiting a man's cheek does not fall under "Eye for an eye"; but in Deut. 25:11 f., where a woman used her hands offensively on a man, "Then cut off her hand." In other words, the insulting party's duty to pay a fine is based on the injunction from Deut. Yet Christ assumed it was based on an eye for an eye when he demanded a man should reply to a slap in the face by offering the other cheek. (He was illustrating an attitude that leaves behind the old principle of talion. If a man attacked another, the Rabbis considered five damages: 1. Compensation for actual damages; 2. Pain; 3. Loss of time by incapacity to work; 4. Cost of healing, fees; and 5. Insult.) The first four are pecuniary and fall under the "Eye for an eye" clause as well as Ex. 21:24-25, wound for wound, stripe for stripe.

But what about indignity? Smiting a man's cheek is a typical case of insult without actual damage to the person. Only in the case of a slap in the face does unlawfulness alone constitute the offense, that is, the violation of another person's rights is in the foreground, not concealed behind concrete facts like a fractured limb or a torn-out eye; a plaintiff could show no physical damage but appealed for redress on the sole ground that a wrong (tort) had been done to him. Unlawfulness presupposes the existence of another person's rights as such, the violation of which, independent of actual damage, entitles him to recompense.

Although actionable, there were technical difficulties in securing redress. There is no obvious provision in the Bible concerning insult, yet in order for any Rabbinical halakha to carry authority, the regulation must have a basis in the Bible and this falls under Deut. 25:11 f. The technical term for *insult* and *shame* has the same root. Hence the Biblical basis for the regulation of the delict of insult was assured. The words "cut off hands" in the original sense were long dead letters, but the Rabbis were determined that the Bible contain no vain provision, and thus became the basis for compensation for insult. The words "cut off hands" referred to monetary compensation. Now the literal "an eye for an eye" was indeed the most serious penalty that ancient legislation could devise, *a fortiori,* all the stronger reason that to "cut off hands" for shame or insult, a case of *a minori ad majus,* infinitely from the less to the greater, should become a dead letter kept alive by the Rabbinic device.

But Jesus looked on the "Eye for eye" provision as the principal governmental compensation in the case of insult. In Rabbinic law the principal was derived from the injunction to "cut off hands." He was unaware of the technical rabbinic analysis of insult as appears in Mishna and Mekilta.

The account that appears in Matthew represents a popular, unlearned view as distinct from academic teaching. When Jesus preached, or the verse was composed, it may be that this technique of dealing with the law of insult was not yet developed. Rabbis themselves regarded the maxim "Eye for an eye" as sufficiently comprehensive to include smiting cheeks as well as breaking arms.

There is a sufficiently satisfactory explanation of the Matthaean passage and the date of its composition. The date was early, before the delict of insult was severed from "Eye" and assigned to "Thou shalt cut off her hand." This is a plain instance where the New Testament has preserved a pre-Talmudic stage of Jewish private law (the law of torts) far removed from the law of the Bible, that is, monetary compensation for insult, as well as for wounds, less advanced than Mishna and Mekilta which distinguish separate texts for actual damage and the law of insult, but basing both actions on "Eye for eye."

III

To reflect on the foregoing brings a sense of deep loss and regret at the opportunities lost for meaningful relations and interaction between the faiths. Yet as written, and popularly understood, the language of the Gospels can only result in what Jules Isaac terms "The Teaching of Contempt."

In 1908 Solomon Schecter wrote: "I have often heard the wish expressed that a history of the rise of Christianity might be written by a Jew who could bring Rabbinic learning to bear upon the subject. I do not think that the time is as yet ripe for such an experiment. The best thing to be done at present is, that Christians devote themselves to the study of Rabbinic literature."[21] While the great scholar's advice should not be lightly regarded, he appears to have disregarded the "blind spot" complex that beclouds the study of Rabbinic literature even among the Dead Sea Scroll scholars.[22] Perhaps the time is still "not yet ripe," but will it ever be? As Hillel put it—"If not now, when?"

81

Coming close to the requirements is the writing of a man I consider among the moving spirits of this century, Rabbi Leo Baeck (1873-1956). The German-Jewish community chose him as the representative to negotiate for them with their Nazi jailers. Baeck accepted this responsibility. He was a constant visitor to Gestapo headquarters fighting for a milder form of anti-Semitism than was being promulgated. The remaining free nations had closed their ears, hearts and doors to the prisoners of the Third Reich and Hitler's bold program grew every day more ominous and feasible. Baeck brought a trainload of children abroad, and despite offers of asylum in England and America, returned to enter the concentration camp with his people. I quote from his masterpiece, *The Essence of Judaism*:[23]

> "As a saying of the Talmud puts it: 'Love God in the human beings whom He has created.' When we seek our brother we find a way to God. The comprehensiveness of this demand was stressed by Hillel, when he declared this inner acknowledgment of our neighbor to be the 'essence of the Torah.' "
>
> "In Judaism there is therefore no piety without the fellow man. The life of the recluse is looked upon as lacking life's most essential feature: service to the brother man. . . . St. Augustine said, God and the soul, and nothing else, 'constitute the whole and true content of religion.' Judaism could not accept this self-centered faith. In the language of Judaism its religious spirit expresses this idea by incorporating the conception of the pious man in the *zaddik*, or 'righteous man'; and in the *hasid*, or 'loving man,' both terms which stress the need to fulfill one's duty to fellow man."
>
> "Our relation to our fellow man is thereby lifted out of the sphere of good will, affection, or even

love; it is exalted into the sphere of the established relationship with God . . . and thereby unites all. . . . And this is a claim which is unconditional. Even our enemy may and must demand the fulfillment of our duty, for though he is our enemy he does not cease to be our fellow man. 'If thine enemy be hungry, give him bread to eat; and if he be thirsty, give him water to drink (Prov. 25:21)."

Here, I gather, is a correct rendition of the Sermon on the Mount without the "but I say" like so many barbs thrust at an adversary.

"If thou meet thine enemy's ox or his ass going astray, thou shalt surely bring it back to him again. If thou see the ass of him that hateth thee lying under his burden, do not forbear to help him, thou shalt surely help him unload the ass" (Exod. 23:4 f.).

"All our duties to our neighbor come under the commandment of justice, the domain of absolute obligation. . . . By this emphasis on our neighbor's right, that which we are bound to grant him is lifted above the transitory emotional impulse and placed on the solid ground of clear duty." [24]

"Thou shalt love thy neighbor as thyself" (Lev. 19:18). "Thou shalt love the stranger as thyself" (Lev. 23:9). In this concept is present the fulfilment of "justice." Through it, our action in behalf of our neighbor is transformed from an external deed in accordance with duty into a deed of our personality.

The Talmud says—"Beneficence and love outweigh all other commandments of the Bible." Nothing in talmudic literature is more emphatically stressed than those two virtues, and most especially the love of our neighbor.—"Love is the beginning and the end of the Torah." "He who withholds love from his brother is like an idolator, like one who rejects the service of God." "This says the Torah: Take upon yourselves the kingdom of heaven, live with one another in the fear of God, and act toward one another in love." "This is the threefold sign of the Israelite: that he is merciful, chaste and loving." [25]

"Do not do unto others as you would not be done by." When he put his maxim into negative form, Hillel had a good reason. For the beginning of all love of man is the resolve not to hurt anyone. The positive follows by itself. If hardly any other virtue so often becomes an empty shell as does the love of our neighbor, it is because we so easily forget what love ought not to do. In the realm of ethics it is the negative which has the hardest limits, the most definite demands; in what we are not to do we learn what we are to do. This is so in every approach to goodness: we begin by averting ourselves from and turning against evil. All love for the great begins with the loathing of the mean.—To do no wrong is the first step to doing right. "To depart from evil is understanding" (Job 28:28). Hence the constant imposing "Thou shalt not" of the Bible. Where that injunction is lacking, everything evaporates into vague enthusiasm and mere talk. "Thou shalt not hate thy brother in thy heart" (Lev. 19:17). For according to the ancient interpretation a hostile feeling already amounts to hatred. [26]

"These last commandments expressly extend the love for neighbor to the enemy. Since the duty of justice is absolute and includes our enemy, we are to help him when he needs our support. This duty to the enemy carries within it a severe tension. My neighbor is my enemy: he is a human being and therefore near to me, but yet he stands against me and is humanly far from me; thus he is far and near simultaneously. I am to consider him as my fellow man yet he does not want to be my fellow man; he is thereby united with and separated from me at the same time. Moreover, the fact that he is an enemy can also signify the most deep-seated antithesis that threatens to tear apart the unity between man and fellow man. I see my enemy before me; that which I spurn in the very depths of my being because it is inhuman, hostile to God, stands before me in him. 'Do not I hate them, O Lord, that hate thee?' (Ps. 139:21). Yet I am to acknowledge humanity in the man of evil and in the enemy of God to find the divine.

"The tension is overcome by the demand for justice. Even though the enemy is a foe of the commandment and therefore not a fellow man, I must not be like him; I must fulfill my life by the justice I mete out to others and thus also to my enemy. Since that duty is absolute and unconditional, my enemy, no matter how much he separates himself from me, is still bound to me in the unity of man and fellow man. Precisely in relation to him do we realize the full strength of the commandment of humanity. That is why, as an old law puts it, duty toward him takes precedence over duty toward a friend. To return evil for evil would mean to deny the commandment enjoined upon us; it would mean that justice was subject to the assumption of our infallibility in inflicting punishment. 'Am I in the place of God?' (Gen.

50:19). 'Say not thou, I will recompense evil; but wait on the Lord and he shall save thee' (Prov. 20:22)."27

"With good reason do these conceptions all begin with the negative, 'Thou shalt not.' 'Thou shalt not take revenge, thou shalt not retaliate' (Lev. 19:18). For only through the negative is the way opened to the positive. Do no wrong to an enemy—that is the beginning. Only on this basis does the love of the enemy not evaporate into empty sentiment."

"To love means first and foremost not to hate.— Always Judaism warns against all unloving and hateful feeling; that is a specific demand and not simply an exaggerated sentiment. 'Rejoice not when thy enemy falls, and let not thine heart be glad when he is overthrown' (Prov. 24:17). The Talmud describes hate as 'baseless' suggesting thereby that the fact that others hate is no reason why we should do the same. As the Talmud also says: 'He who hates stands with those who shed blood.' 28

"Talmud: 'Of those who are oppressed and do not oppress, who are reviled and who do not in turn revile, who act only from love, and gladly bear their sufferings, the Scripture says, 'They who love Him are like the sun when it rises in its might.'

"The crusaders killed the wife and child of Eleazar ben Judah of Worms and wounded him almost to the point of death. Yet when as an old man he recorded his experiences he wrote not one word of hatred against his enemies. He insisted even then that it is better to suffer wrong than to do it." 29

"The great test of genuineness in love is love for the enemy; through it love's purity and sincerity are most thoroughly revealed. Much more easily than justice can love become insincere. It is easy for love

86

to lose itself in empty emotionalism or hypocrisy—
truth has a social quality. Not only does God demand it, not only does our soul demand it; our fellow man has the right to demand it, for we owe it to
him as a human obligation." [30]

"The fact that in the Gospels neighborly love appears as a quotation from the Old Testament is sufficient to refute the attempts that have often been
made to rank its expression in the Torah and by the
prophets as below that of Christianity. Nor does it
require elaboration to show how love is limited and
confined in the New Testament by the fact that salvation and bliss are made dependent upon right
faith and thereby ultimately upon dogma and creed.
This means that salvation and bliss are denied to a
section of even the best brother-men, the 'non-be-
lievers.' It is in the range allowed to the conception
of salvation that a religion's humanity, its inner ac-
knowledgment of the fellow man, is most decisively
expressed. But in Christianity the determining factor
is to experience the miracle of grace and thereby be
redeemed; thus the 'I' of the individual man stands
alone at the center of religion, apart from the fellow
man." [31]

Many questions leap to mind at Rabbi Baeck's discourse,
but most would be impudent in view of the living testament
to his faith that he leaves us. Most of the misunderstand-
ings would be clarified if Torah were not mistranslated "the
law" as, for example, in the Epistles of St. Paul, rather than
more correctly "the Teaching." [32] Baeck was not conducting
a course in jurisprudence but in revelation of the Divine
Commandment. But perhaps it would not be impertinent to
raise some general observations.

Why, for instance, should the millennial pursuit of absolute justice be the distinctive Jewish vocation among the peoples of the earth? Why elevate a historical predicament into an eternal imperative? Despite St. Paul, Pascal, and Kierkegaard, the evidence, on the whole, indicates that it is not granted to most human beings to identify with all mankind in one grand leap of the imagination.

It is hardly possible to do more than contend with a problem on the historical level. Avoiding the route of the Messianic escape, the Zionists have not been afraid to undertake historical responsibility, and therein lies their greatness.

Judaism exists but is difficult to define. There is less need to define it than to decide whether we wish to alter it or continue it. Simply, a living thing is not amenable to dogmatic definition. It contains and continues a vital force. Can there be the creation of forms belonging to holiness with universal significance? It is still given to discover exalted things which no one has yet beheld.

The rebuilding of the nation may explain the mystical meaning of the secret of the universe. Judaism, while not based on a system of articles of faith, is a life lived in faith, depending on Divinity while the rest of the world believes in and depends on the natural law.

Finally, there is no yawning gulf, no unbridgeable chasm, between the message of the Sermon on the Mount and fundamental Judaism. Our study, if it has done anything, has proved the truth of Paul's conclusion (Rom. 11:16-20): "If the root is holy, so are the branches. But if some of the branches were broken off, and you, a wild olive shoot, were grafted in their place to share the richness of the olive tree, do not boast over the branches. If you do boast, remember it is not you that supports the root, but the root that supports you. So do not become proud but stand in awe."

Notes to
The Sermon
and the Synagogue

1. Abba Hille Silver, *Where Judaism Differed* (New York: The Macmillan Company, 1956) pp. 304, 306, 307.
2. Ibid., p. 308, citing the Talmud, Berakoth 58a. Note that this case is derived by the Rabbis from Ex. 22:1, which declares it legitimate to kill a burglar who is prepared to commit murder.
3. Dictionary of the History of Ideas, ed. Philip Wiener. (New York: Charles Scribner's Sons, 1973) Vol. III pp. 440–41. See also Hyam Muccoby, *Revolution in Judaea,* op. cit., p. 110.
4. Talmud, Gittin, 56b. See *The Jewish Encyclopedia* Vol. VII p. 18.
5. W.D. Davies, *The Setting of the Sermon on the Mount* (Cambridge: Cambridge University Press, 1963) p. 286. This study is significant in its use of early Judaism in interpreting the Sermon.
6. Boston: Beacon Press, 1962.
7. *Pharisaic* is defined by the Oxford English Dictionary as "being strict in doctrine and ritual, without the spirit of piety; laying stress upon the outward show of re-

ligion and morality, and assuming superiority on that account; hypocritical; formal; self-righteous."
Although the line between academic freedom and slander is not formally delineated, that need not lead to an utter abandonment of scholarship.
That same immobile dictionary, despite innumerable protests and petitions, persists in defining a *Jew* as "a grasping or extortionate usurer, or trader who drives hard bargains or deals craftily, that is a Jew, as *Jew boy* etc." The verb Jew is "to cheat or overreach."

8. Herford, op. cit., p. 208.
9. Ibid., p. 209.
10. See Robert Graves and Joshua Podro, *The Nazarene Gospel Restored* (Garden City: Doubleday & Company, Inc. 1954), p. 151.
11. Herford, op. cit., p. 209.
12. Paul Winter, *On the Trial of Jesus* (Berlin: Walter de Gruyter & Company, 1961), p. 133. See p. 45 supra. For an interesting examination of the hostility in the Gospels to Pharisees instead of to his actual opponents the Scribes see Morton Smith, *Jesus The Magician* (New York: Harper & Row, 1978), p. 30 ff. and Appendix A. See also Hyam Maccoby, op. cit., p. 98.
13. W.D. Davies, op. cit., p. 315.
14. For the Rabbinic analysis of this section I am indebted to Professor David Daube, *The New Testament and Rabbinic Judaism*, (London: The Athlone Press, 1956), p. 255 ff. and Gerald Friedlander, *The Jewish Sources of the Sermon on The Mount* (New York: KTAV Publishing House, Inc., 1969, first published in 1911). The legal material is contained in tractate Baba Kamma 83b to 93a, The Talmud.
15. For approximation of the dating see James Parkes, *The Foundations of Judaism and Christianity* (Chicago:

Quadrangle Books, 1960), p. 79 and references. As for the Talmudic reasoning involved see Kethuboth 32b.
16. The Babylonian Talmud (London: The Soncino Press, 1935).
17. Ibid., Berakoth 43b.
18. Ibid., Sanhedrin 58b.
19. Ibid., Baba Kamma 93a.
20. Ibid., Baba Kamma 92a.
21. *Studies in Judaism,* (New York: Meridian Books, Inc. 1958), p. 71.
22. Supra, p. 35.
23. (New York: Schocken Books, 1948), p. 193 f.
24. Ibid., pp. 194-5.
25. Ibid., p. 211.
26. Ibid., p. 212.
27. Ibid., p. 213.
28. Ibid., p. 214.
29. Ibid., p. 216.
30. Ibid., p. 217.
31. Ibid., p. 222.
32. See, e.g., Martin Buber, *Two Types of Faith* (New York: Harper & Row, 1961), p. 57.

TWO BOOKS

Clement of Alexandria and
a Secret Gospel of Mark

BY MORTON SMITH

The Sacred Mushroom and the Cross

BY JOHN M. ALLEGRO

I
Clement of Alexandria and a Secret Gospel of Mark
BY MORTON SMITH

The Background

In the summer of 1958 Morton Smith, professor of Ancient History at Columbia University, spent a fortnight at the Monastery of Mar Saba, located in the Judean desert, a few miles southeast of Jerusalem. Among the items he examined and catalogued was a manuscript of two and a half pages of writing (reproduced at the back of an old printed book). The heading reads: "From the letters of the most holy Clement, the author of the Stromateis; to Theodore." Then comes the text of the letter.

Professor Smith documented his discovery in a book: "Clement of Alexandria and a Secret Gospel of Mark."

This was published in 1973 by the Harvard University Press. Professor Smith spends an entire section of his book examining the *bona fides* and authenticity of the manuscript and concludes, not unreasonably, that the document truly derives from the pen of Clement of Alexandria (born circa 150 A.D.), early church father. The letter is Clement's reply to an unknown Theodore, who had opposed the teachings of the Carpocratians, a libertine gnostic sect, and was concerned by their claim to be in possession of a longer Gospel written by Mark. Clement states that Mark did indeed write a longer Gospel—a secret Gospel used by the Alexandrian church for the initiation of Christians into its mysteries. He declares the Carpocratians' text was a stolen and corrupted version of the text belonging to the Alexandrian church. Clement quotes two passages from the Secret Gospel which affirm that Jesus administered a baptism consisting of a nocturnal initiation, and another describing a conflict between Jesus, the Marys and Salome.

The bulk of Smith's treatise is an explanation of these passages in light of the secret and libertine elements of the early church as reflected in Jesus' teaching. There is a process described by Smith and his late colleague Moses Hadas as "aretalogy," "not recognized as a word in our dictionaries." (It is defined as a narrative of the miraculous deeds of a god or hero.) The documents called aretalogical, though possessing high importance for religious development, have not commonly had their history and internal relationships presented as a separate unity.[1] If I follow them correctly, I gladly avail myself of this technique to present Smith's own considerable discoveries to a public he may not have intended to confront. The work is replete (the word repellent is almost more suitable) with a scholarship so dense as to discourage all but the most hardy and seaworthy passengers. Yet his conclusions are simple, straightforward and entirely convincing. But it will not do to leap baldly to conclusions. One is required to take the voyage, see the pitfalls, the landscape, the perils before safe harbor is sighted. The esthetics and logic of the situation must be met fairly. One does not read the last page of his favorite mystery writer and cluck, "I told you so." The struggle on the author's terms must be met.

The other book of which I speak, *The Sacred Mushroom and the Cross*,[2] is a vastly different product. John Allegro, going beyond New Testament scholarship, has devoted himself to a study of philology. "Now we face a new revolution in thought which must make us reconsider the validity of the New Testament story. Our fresh doubts about the historicity of Jesus and his friends stem not from new discoveries about the land and people of Palestine of the first century, but about the nature and origin of the languages they spoke and the origins of their religious cults."[3]

"The fungus recognized today as the *Aminita Muscaria*, or Fly-Agaric, has been known from the beginning of history."[4] "Those mushroom epithets and holy invocations that the Christian cryptographers wove into their stories of the man Jesus and his companions can now be recognized, and the main features of the Christian cult laid bare."[5]

Civilization began in Sumer, in the land of the Two Rivers, Mespotamia. "Yet a century ago no one had ever heard of the Sumerians. About the middle of the 19th Century Sir Henry Rawlinson and others deciphered Accadian cuneiform on the basis of a trilingual inscription. Some of the tablets had another quite unknown tongue, interspersed between the lines. These were the Sumers, a pre-Semitic population from whom the Assyrians had borrowed the art of writing."

John M. Allegro, a lecturer in Old Testament and Inter-Testamental studies at the University of Manchester, was appointed to an international team editing the Dead Sea Scrolls for publication and published a book on the Scrolls.[6]

His approach to the New Testament is that of a cryptographer. He finds names that are deliberately mistranslated so that if the testament falls into unfriendly hands, the chances that they could be correctly identified are nil. At the same time there was no possibility that the mistranslation would deceive or mislead any of the initiates to whom the mysteries were revealed.

With such vastly differering approaches, both scholars, dealing with the same material, arrive at much the same conclusions. A small corner of the curtain of a hitherto impenetrable mystery has been drawn back. No one could have foreseen such stunning results. "The content of this text is so surprising, that if Clement really was its author the consequences for the history of the early Christian church and for New Testament criticism are revolutionary," writes Smith.

"The isolation of the mushroom cult and the real hidden meaning of the New Testament writings drives a wedge between the moral teachings of the Gospels and their quite amoral religious settings" (Allegro).[7] "Above all, it is the philologian who must be the spearhead of the new enquiry. It is primarily a study in words."[8] As the late Harry Austryn Wolfson put it: "There is sleuthing in scholarship, as there is in crime, and it is as full of mystery, danger, intrigue, suspense, and thrills—if only the story were told."[9]

Reviewing the writing of both scholars one is reminded of the technique of Freud in his work on dream analysis. What is presented on the surface level of both New Testament writing and dream content is the "manifest" material that is presented in its vivid realistic appearance. As one penetrates the surface, it becomes apparent that the "manifest" material has been subjected to an immense distortion by the dynamics of the dream mechanism: symbolism, compression, displacement, substitution, reversal. When one has decoded all the censorship involved, it is possible to arrive at what Freud calls the *latent* content. It is from the latent content or "dream-thoughts" and not from a dream's manifest content that we disentangle its meaning. To attempt to derive meaning from the manifest content instead of according to their symbolic relation, we should clearly be led into error.

In their illuminating ways, both scholars discount the manifest surface stories projected by the New Testament and penetrate to the mysterious world of the hidden meaning that enriches and enlightens our thinking on these all-absorbing subjects.

A breakthrough in scholarship means a breakthrough in understanding, no matter how remote a letter by Clement of Alexandria, or how very far the Sumer hieroglyphics may seem from our ordinary day to day interests. Who, in his wildest imagination, would guess that a professor of history from Columbia University on a sabbatical in Jerusalem would uncover an unknown Gospel of Mark in the Judean desert; or that a gentle lecturer from the University of Manchester would trace the Sumer roots of the sacred mushroom cult in the texts of the Old and New Testaments? We must face the implications of these discoveries as our ancestors faced Galileo's pronouncements, Newton's laws, and Darwin's theory.

A word of warning. The method of Smith is pragmatic, scientific. He prepares a demonstration and is quite willing and anxious to modify his conclusions if error, omission or new findings are discovered which throw light on his subject. Allegro, on the other hand, proceeds deductively from premise to conclusion, and is subject to quite a different order of criticism. Take, for example, the noun *testimony:* It is derived from the Latin root *testis,* the male reproductive organ. For its possible ancient derivation see Gen. 24:2, 3. Now suppose our civilization were to be uncovered some four thousand years hence and a clever philologist of the future were to derive this word and trace it to its sexual root. Poring through our court records, legal procedures and law libraries, he might get some peculiar ideas of a widespread fertility cult. The point need not be pressed, as the comparison is not entirely fair. The nature of a cryptogram is to prevent its message and meaning from coming to public attention. Allegro points out that false translations are inserted in the New Testament to accomplish precisely this result, and scholarship alone is of no avail until a key to the cryptogram is provided. It is just this key that Allegro believes his studies have provided.

The Fragment
Translation of the Text

From the letters of the most holy Clement, the author of the Stromateis. To Theodore.

You did well in silencing the unspeakable teachings of the Carpocratians. For these are the "wandering stars" referred to in the prophecy, who wander from the narrow road of the commandments into a boundless abyss of the carnal and bodily sins. For, priding themselves in knowledge, as they say, "of the deep things of Satan," they do not know that they are casting themselves away into "the nether world of the darkness" of falsity, and, boasting that they are free, they have become slaves of servile desires. Such men are to be opposed in all ways and altogether. For, even if they should say something true, one who loves the truth should not, even so, agree with them. For not all true things are the truth, nor should that truth which merely seems true according to human opinions be preferred to the true truth, that according to the faith.

Now of the things they keep saying about the divinely inspired Gospel according to Mark, some are altogether falsifications, and others, even if they do contain some true elements, nevertheless are not reported truly. For the true things being mixed with inventions, are falsified, so that, as the saying goes, even the salt loses its savor.

As for Mark, then, during Peter's stay in Rome he wrote an account of the Lord's doings, not, however, declaring all of them, nor yet hinting at the secret ones, but selecting what he thought most useful for increasing the faith of those who were being instructed. But when Peter died a martyr, Mark came over to Alexandria, bringing both his own notes and those of Peter, from which he transferred to his former book the things suitable to whatever makes for progress toward knowledge. Thus he composed a more spiritual Gospel for the use of those who were being perfected. Nevertheless, he yet did not divulge the things not to be uttered, nor did he write down the hierophantic teaching of the Lord, but to the stories already written he added yet others and, moreover, brought in certain sayings of which he knew the interpretation would, as a mystagogue, lead the hearers into the innermost sanctuary of that truth hidden by seven veils. Thus, in sum, he prepared matters, neither grudgingly nor incautiously, in my opinion, and, dying, he left his composition to the church in Alexandria, where it even yet is most carefully guarded, being read only to those who are being initiated into the great mysteries. But since the foul demons are always devising destruction for the race of men, Carpocrates, instructed by them and using deceitful arts, so enslaved a certain presbyter of the church in Alexandria that he got from him a copy of the secret Gospel, which he both interpreted according to his blasphemous and carnal doctrine and, moreover, polluted, mixing with the spotless and holy words utterly shameless lies. From this mixture is drawn off the teaching of the Carpocratians.

To them, therefore, as I have said above, one must never give way; nor, when they put forward their falsifications, should one concede that the secret Gospel is by Mark, but should even deny it on oath. For, "Not all true things are to be said to all men." For this reason the Wisdom of God, through Solomon, advises, "Answer the fool from his folly," teaching that the light of the truth should be hidden from those who are mentally blind. Again it says, "From him who has not shall be taken away," and, "Let the fool walk in darkness." But we are "children of light" having been illuminated by "the dayspring" of the spirit of the Lord "from on high," and "Where the Spirit of the Lord is," it says, "there is liberty," for "All things are pure to the pure." To you, therefore, I shall not hesitate to answer the questions you have asked, refuting the falsifications by the very words of the Gospel. For example, after "And they were in the road going up to Jerusalem," and what follows, until "After three days he shall arise," the secret Gospel brings the following material word for word: "And they come into Bethany. And a certain woman whose brother had died was there. And, coming, she prostrated herself before Jesus and says to him, 'Son of David, have mercy on me.' But the disciples rebuked her. And Jesus, being angered, went off with her into the garden where the tomb was, and straightway a great cry was heard from the tomb. And going near Jesus rolled away the stone from the door of the tomb. And straightway, going in where the youth was, he stretched forth his hand and raised him, seizing his hand. But the youth, looking upon him, loved him and began to beseech him that he might be with him. And going out of the tomb they came into the house of the youth, for he was rich. And after six days Jesus told him what to do and in the evening the youth comes to him, wearing a linen cloth over his naked body. And he remained with him that night, for Jesus taught him the mystery of the kingdom of God. And thence, arising, he returned to the other side of the Jordan." After these words follows the text, "And James and John come to him," and all that section. But "naked man with naked man," and the other things about which you wrote, are not found.

And after the words, "And he comes into Jericho," the secret Gospel adds only, "And the sister of the youth whom Jesus loved and his mother and Salome were there, and Jesus did not receive them." But the many other things about which you wrote both seem to be and are falsifications.

Now the true explanation and that which accords with the true philosophy. . . .

(Here the fragment ends).

The Book

The letter has revealed that Clement's church in Alexandria kept this Gospel secret and read it only to those being initiated into the "great mysteries." The text reports that Jesus administered to one of his followers a nocturnal initiation in which "Jesus taught him the mystery of the kingdom of God." Clement believed that in the Christian tradition was an *unwritten* tradition for the instruction of the gnostic. Clement claimed there was a secret body of doctrine revealed by Christ to Peter, James, and John and handed down orally to Clement's own time. This secret doctrine is not the ordinary ecclesiastical tradition, but is linked with a special Christian initiation by which it is communicated not to all Christians but to a chosen few.

Clement has been called "liberal" possibly because of his ambivalent attitude toward gnosticism, i.e. violent abuse of gnostics with claims to enjoy the true gnosis and possess the true secret doctrine. This concern disappears after the middle of the third century when interest is focused on the trinitarian controversy. The source of his gnosis, a secret oral tradition derived from Jesus, contains the highest truth which can be revealed only to the gnostic. The tradition should be hidden, not only from outsiders, but from neophytes and unworthy Christians. It is a Christian's duty to conceal the truth. Clement makes it clear that he has no intention of writing down the innermost secrets.

It appeared that some of this secret doctrine had been written down and some of these written works had fallen into the hands of the unworthy—the heretics, the gnostics and the libertines. Of libertine gnostics, the sect of most concern to Clement are the Carpocratians. The Carpocratians were annihilated by a great persecution (202 A.D.) which also drove Clement out of Alexandria. Origen, one generation later, never met a Carpocratian.

In the letter, surprise is expressed at information about Mark's secret Gospel and the Carpocratian corruption of it. The letter presents this as confidential and directs that Markan authorship of the secret Gospel (or the Carpocratian secret Gospel) is to be denied on oath. It follows that we should not find this information in his published works. He thought concealment of truth to be part of his Christian duty.

The letter says the doctrines of Carpocrates are derived from the secret Gospel of Mark which Carpocrates got from a presbyter of the church in Alexandria for those being initiated into its "great mysteries."

The longer text taken together with Mk. 10:20-32 suggests that the longer text was originally part of the Gospel. The action in Mk. 10:21 is attributed to Jesus ("And Jesus looking upon him loved him") and the longer text (2 recto 4) to the youth in the tomb ("But the youth, looking upon him, loved him"). In Mt. 19:20 the same man asks Jesus "What do I still lack?"

We identify this man with the youth in the longer text: the youth looking at Jesus, loved him, *and therefore* begged to be with him, *and therefore* the two of them went to the youth's house (for he was rich). It is notable that Mt. 19:20

makes the unidentified rich man of Mk. a "youth" without the possibly objectionable attribution to Jesus of love for a man.

A modification of Mark of abandonment of property as a requirement for baptism is softened in Mt. 19:22 to a counsel of perfection. No survival of this requirement appears in the baptismal teaching of the later church.

In the baptismal service the preliminary instructions in monotheism, the commandments, and charity which Christianity had in common with Judaism, is followed by the prophecy of the passion and resurrection, the essential of the specifically Christian creed.

The Savior entering the tomb reaches his hand to the dead (Jesus opens the tomb himself—against John)—and (probably) raises Lazarus by hand. The Lazarus story (John and Mark) was connected with baptismal resurrection. John prefaces his version by a contrast of Jesus with the Baptist. The intention may be to contrast the miraculous resurrection effected by the Christian baptism with Johannite baptism which, John implies, had no such supernatural effect. A similar contrast is made in Acts 19: 1-7.

The baptismal concern makes it probable that the nocturnal initiation which follows the Lazarus story should be understood to be a baptism. Baptism is noctural in Acts 16:33. Foot washing (a variant) in Jn. 13 is nocturnal. Nicodemus, Jn. 3, comes to Jesus by night and receives instruction concerning baptism as the means of entering the kingdom of God.

Nudity in baptism is prescribed by Hippolytus (c. 160), Apostolic tradition (xxi 3, 5, 11), also by Rabbinic law proselyte baptism and purification (Yebamoth 47b.). "The early Christian neophyte was baptized completely naked and by the submersion of the body, thereby symbolizing a complete divestment of one's former self and the acquisition of a wholly new state of being."[10]

Jn. 13 for the footwashing rite, Jesus is naked except for

a towel. The begger in Mk. 10:50 throws away his cloak (or
himation) when he comes to Jesus to be cured. Naked baptism was already customary in Paul's time. Col. 2:11; Gal.
3:27; I Cor. 15:33 and II Cor. 5:2. In Mk. 14:51 the young
man with Jesus at the time of his arrest was seized and fled
naked. (Mat. and Lk. omit.) The youth had come to be
baptized.

The white garment had some special significance in the
early church. The garment was baptismal and burial garment, and also the resurrection garment.

Mk. 4:11, "To you has been given the secret of the kingdom of God, but for those outside everything is in parables; so they may indeed see but not perceive, and may
indeed hear but not understand."

The compiler of Mark knew the logia as addressed to
Jesus' circle, for it is something which already "Has been
given" in the past, something which Jesus' intimates have
already received and which makes it possible for Jesus to
give them now, as a further gift, the explanation of the
parable. The "mystery" which "was given" to members of
the Church, which distinguished them from non-members,
and which enabled them to be given the secret teachings of
the Church, was baptism.

The "mystery" is presumably the spiritual union effected
by baptism and thence the rite itself which makes the
Church the body of Christ by making Christ's spirit live in
the members. The use of "mystery" to refer to baptism is
found in I Cor. 2:6 f.

Ephesians 5: 28-32 makes the Church the body of Christ.
It compares the mystery to the spiritual union effected by
physical intercourse in marriage—of two one flesh—
Gen. 2:24.

The "wisdom of God" (I Cor. 2:7) is revealed in baptism
for it involves the secret of Christ's descent in disguise and
his assumption of the body from the cosmic powers, for the

purpose of subjugating them. This secret of descent in disguise structures Paul's interpretation of baptism in Col. 2:15, where the second half of the process, the stripping off in the ascent, is referred to. The conclusion of the process in I Cor. 2:9 as in Co. 2:12; 3:4, is the participation of the baptized in Christ's resurrection, ascension and session in glory. Therefore the mystery is baptism.

Conclusion: The longer text was the original text of Mark and the canonical text was produced by abbreviation. In 10:46 the present text seems to be an abridgment and the longer text quoted by Clement preserves the introductory phrases of the material that has been cut out.

The cry from the tomb would have led many ancient readers to question the miracle—stories of persons who were thought to have died but came back to life were frequently in antiquity (Plato, *Republic* 614); and the notion the persons "raised" by Jesus had not really been dead was a frequent embarrassment to Christian apologists. Embarrassment was already felt by John and John emphasized the four days entombment so they should not have any ground to disbelieve that the man whom Jesus raised had been dead (Chrysostom). John suppressed the voice from the tomb and transferred the loud voice to Jesus in spite of the fact that it is somewhat out of character.

The letter has revealed that Clement's church in Alexandria kept this Gospel secret and read it only to those being initiated into the "great mysteries." The text reports that Jesus administered to one of his followers a nocturnal initiation in which "Jesus taught him the mystery of the kingdom of God."

Stories of this same form—pronouncement, question in private, secret teaching to disciples—are in Mark 4:10 ff; 7:17 ff; 9:28 ff; 10:10 ff; 13:3 ff. The tradition is that Jesus *did* teach in secret and this tradition was older than the Gospels.

Jesus' claim in his trial (Jn 18:20), "I have said nothing secretly," probably reflects a charge of secret teaching, yet John represents Nicodemus as coming for secret instruction by night, also that Joseph of Arimathea was a secret disciple, 19:38, and makes the last supper a secret lecture.

This is reflected in Paul, I Cor. 2:11, and there is no doubt that Paul had secret teachings which he will not reveal even to baptized Christians who are still "carnal" (3:1 ff).

In sum, the Gospels all represent Jesus as teaching in secret. When Christianity first appears in the writings of pagan authors it is described as a secret society or an initiation.

Content of Jesus' Secret Teaching

There is no scholarly agreement as to what he taught in public. Represented as a rabbi, a philosopher, a pacifist, a revolutionary, a moral reformer, and the son of God come down to earth to reveal his own nature, the fact is that the canonical Gospels contain elements which give contradictory pictures, contradictions dealt with by supposing one body of material "primary" and the rest "secondary," producing the various "historical" pictures of Jesus. Or they may be reconciled by considerations that have not been made public. Mk. 4:33, he did not speak to them without a parable, but privately to his own disciples he explained everything.

To the question: "What did Jesus tell his disciples in darkness?" the answer has usually been "the messianic secret." It seems likely that Jesus did think he was the Messiah and had obvious, prudential reasons to conceal his opinion.

On the other hand there is no reason to suppose Jesus had only one secret—the notion that he was the Messiah.

Mk. 4:11 declares that "the mystery of the Kingdom of God" has been given to the disciples and the new text represents Jesus as teaching this mystery to the youth who came to him for nocturnal initiation. The evidence indicates that the mystery was a baptism.

Christianity according to the New Testament begins with John the Baptist (Mk. 1:1 ff; Lk. 16:16; Mt. 11:12 f). The New Testament is confirmed by Josephus, who had heard of John as a figure influential and popular (A. J. XVIII 116 ff).

To understand the innovation of the new rite instituted by John one must realize the distinction in Jewish law between sin and impurity. Impurity was removed by immersions, but sin only by the expiatory rites and prayers of the Day of Atonement. To introduce a new rite effective for the remission of all sins was a great innovation. It had to be administered by the Baptist or one of his disciples and was not connected with any teaching about the holy spirit. By John's time the only place in Palestine where Jews could legally offer sacrifices was in Jerusalem, a situation which was burdensome and expensive.

Jesus' use of baptism is obscure. Nothing is said of his having baptized his followers in the synoptics. In the Fourth Gospel he did baptize, then did not baptize, but his disciples did. In Mk. 1:8 the Baptist is made to declare that he can baptize only with water but his greater successor will baptize with the holy spirit. But this may be a polemic against his followers. Smith believed that Jesus did baptize.

The Baptist preached repentance and conducted himself as a penitent, but Jesus "came eating and drinking" (Lk. 7:34; Mt. 11:19). Jesus compared his followers to the members of a bridal party (Mk. 2:18). He justified their laxity by comparing them to the companions of David (Mk. 2:25). Jesus was not a preacher of repentance. He forgave sins without demanding repentance (Mk. 2:5) and thus differed fundamentally from the Baptist. The right to forgive sins (claimed by Jesus) is to possess a dignity equal to Yahweh (Mk. 2:5,6,7).

The emphasis of the Gospels is that Jesus was not merely a prophet (Mk. 8:28; Lk. 7:26; Mt. 11:9; Jn. 4:19-26). It would seem that the function of Jesus somehow enabled some of his followers to enter the kingdom forthwith and in some special fashion other than repentance and obedience to the law which would make them greater than the Baptist, give them power over demons and diseases, and admit them at once to the feast.

Jesus effected the admission of his chosen followers by some sort of baptism. John the Baptist's rite did not admit the recipient to the kingdom, but Jesus' did. It differed in being not only private but secret.

The earliest Christian documents on baptism are Paul's letter, about A.D. 50. John's baptism was analogous to biblical and rabbinic immersion, except that it removed sin, whereas they had removed impurity. The baptism of Paul was a means of uniting with the Messiah (Romans 6). The union with the Messiah involves participation in his death and resurrection. The resurrection has already begun. In Galatians 3, "You have clothed yourselves in Messiah" suggests that the baptism was naked. Col. 2:3 indicates that union with the Messiah involves participation in his nature, death, and resurrection. There is a recurrence of the stripping motif in 2:11, 15 and 3:9.

The essential notion of Paul is that baptism results in the possession of the baptized by the spirit of Jesus. Smith suggests that Pauline baptism came specifically from Jesus. It was a means of uniting with Jesus. The union was effected by the Spirit which Jesus had.

Attempts have been made to derive the origin of Pauline baptism from pagan mysteries but the analogies are closest to material found in the magical papyri. The eucharist is another ritual means of uniting with Jesus (eat my body! drink my blood!) almost certainly introduced by Jesus which exemplifies magical practice. This magic is standard procedure in Osiris, Isis blood ritual. Both the baptism and the eucharist are utterly incompatible with rabbinic Judaism.

The Dionysiac myth referred to wine as blood, but in Jesus' eucharist he identifies *his own* blood with wine and gives it to his followers to drink in order to unite them with himself. This goes completely beyond the pagan mysteries and is paralleled only in magic. These two rites of baptism and eucharist break utterly with Judaic practice, are of very early Christian practice; both were introduced by Jesus and both derive from the same type of magical practice.

The spirit first comes into connection with baptism at the baptism of Jesus. All traditions agree on this point. The descent of the spirit on Jesus gives him power to bestow it on others. The spirit possessed him and *drove* him into the wilderness to be tempted by the devil. Jesus acquired a reputation by casting out spirits. He gave his disciples power over spirits. Demons could recognize Jesus but men could not (Mk. 3:11, 1:24, 34). Spirits played such an important role in Jesus' career and since baptism had been the occasion when he was seized by a spirit, he established the rite which transformed baptism into a regular means of giving his initiates a spirit.

Magic

In the Roman Empire the practice of magic was a criminal offense (Paulus, *Sentiae* V. 23.14-18). The Essenes attached great importance to curative magic and Franz Cumont believes the Jews acquired skills in this art from the Persians and Chaldeans.[11]

Jewish magic is mentioned in the Bible (Deut 18:10-11) as well as exorcists and diviners, their ceremonies being forbidden as idolatrous. The commonest form of magic was the love charm, so that magic and adultery are combined (II Kings 9:23; Nah. 3:4; Mal. 3:5). It was associated with vice and sexual license.

In post-biblical times it was only the practice of witchcraft which was prohibited, for a knowledge of magic was indispensable to a member of the council or judiciary. The law did not deny its power. Scholars occasionally counteracted black magic by white. Exorcism was practiced, though not so widely as in Jewish-Christian circles (Acts 8:9; 13:6-9). Jesus was regarded generally as a magician (Sanhedrin 106 b; Sotah 47 b).

According to Celsus (Origen, *Contra Celsum* i 28) and the Talmud (Shab. 104 b) Jesus learned magic in Egypt. The accusation of. magic is frequently brought against Jesus, (Jerome "Ep. lv. ad Ascellam" i 196). Marcus of the Valentinians was, according to Jerome, a native of Egypt, and was accused of being, like Jesus, a magician, while in Rome all Christians were accused of magic.

The efficacy of magic was almost universally believed, and the magician was conceived as a man who, by acquiring supernatural powers, had become a potential danger to the established authorities. "Magician" was a term of abuse.

Thus Jesus is not represented by the Gospels as a magician. He is the Son of God in disguise. The Synoptics never call Jesus "God." John is less inhibited and calls him "Only Begotten God" as distinct from "God" (the Father) 1:18.[12] But his practices were those of contemporary magic. The first suspicious item is that he is represented as a supernatural being—a common claim of magicians. In the *Mithra Liturgy* the magician begins with a prayer that the supreme being will "breathe into me the holy spirit" and then declares, "I am the Son." The main notion of the prayer is that by union with the ruler of gods the initiate can attain superiority to the astral deities, precisely that of Paul in Col. 2:8-3:4.

The Gospels represent Jesus as the Son of God and credit him with the power to perform his miracles immediately. Thus he does not use charms, formulae or special rituals, and this might be thought to distinguish him from the magician, who is supposed to have used on every occasion the elaborate ceremonies of the magical papyri. But many of the ceremonies in the magical papyri are initiations, means of getting a spirit. Once one has a spirit, no such rites are necessary. That Jesus did believe he owed his powers to the possession of such a spirit is strongly suggested by the story of his dying cry, "My God, my God, why hast thou forsaken me?" (Mk. 14:50; Gospel of Peter 19 reads "my *dynamis*" equivalent to "my daimon"). From Mk. 14:50 and 15:40 it seems unlikely that any of Jesus' disciples was on hand to hear what—if anything—he actually said. The reported cry (Ps. 22:2) is their notion of what he should have said—an expression of messianic hope and magical Christology.[13]

Both Mt and Lk omit the saliva miracles of Mk (7:32 ff; 8:22 ff).

The essential content of the Gospel comes from the world of magic.[14] Jesus, like Apollonius, was driven by the spirit into the wilderness, where he was approached by an evil spirit but repulsed it. This accords with the general pattern of shamanic initiation. So does the tradition which represents Jesus as now possessing spirits, and then as himself possessed (Mk. 1:12 f; 3:21-30; Mt. 9:34; 10:25; Jn. 7:20; 8:48 f; 10:20). They are distinguished from ordinary preachers by their miraculous powers. Most of the miracles reported of Jesus are those which are commonly reported of magicians and for which recipes are given in the magical papyri.

The following references appear in the Gospels which are common in magical material:

The power to make anyone he wanted follow him. Mk. 1:16 ff; 2:14.
Exorcism. Mk. 1:23, 34; 3:11, 22; 5:1 ff.
Exorcism at a distance. Mk. 7:25 ff; Lk. 7:1-10.
Miraculous cures. Mk. 1:29 ff, 34, 40 ff; 3:10; 5:25 ff; Lk. 7:18 ff.
Stilling storms. Mk. 4.35 ff; Mk. 4.41.
Raising the dead. Mk. 5:21-43; Lk. 7:11 ff.
Giving his disciples power over demons. Mk. 6:7
Miraculous provision of food. Mk. 6:35 ff; 8:1 ff.
Walking on water. Mk. 6:48.
Miraculous escapes (his body could not be seized) Lk. 4:30; Jn. 7:30, 44; 8:20, 59.
Making himself invisible. Jn. 8:59, 12:36; Lk. 24:31.
Possession of the keys of the kingdom. Mt. 16:19. (The Mithraic Kronos holds in each hand a key as the monarch of the heavens whose portals he opens.[15])
Foreknowledge. Mk. 8:31 ff; Lk. 10:13 f; 13:34 f; 23:28 11; Mk. 13:2; Mk. 5:39; Jn. 11:11 ff; Mk. 14:13 ff.
Knowledge of other's thoughts. Mk. 2:8; 12:15.
Metamorphosis. Mk. 9:3.
Revealing supernatural beings to his disciples. Mk. 9:4.
Prescribing reforms of temple practices. Mk. 11:15 ff.
Introducing a new rite, a meal by which his followers are united with him by partaking of food magically identified with his flesh and blood. Mk. 14:22 ff; Jn. 6:56; I Cor. 10:16; 11:24 f.
Claiming to be united with his disciples, so that he is

in them and they in him. Jn. 6:56; 14:20 15:3 ff, 9.
Claiming to be a god or a son of a god, or united
with some god or supernatural entity (notably in
statements beginning "I am"). Mk. 14:62; 13, 6;

Mt. 26:63; Jn. 10:36; 8:12; 17:21.

The *stories* of the Gospel are mostly stories about things
a magician would do. They are not stories about things the
Messiah would do (exorcism or being eaten). Jesus, like
Apollonius, was involved in arguments about the proper
observance of religious laws. He was thought to be a
prophet and probably came to think himself the Messiah,
but neither his messianic nor legal and prophetic opinions
account for the stories about him, which are stories of a
man who did the things magicians claimed to do. This was
recognized in antiquity even by Christian apologists—Justin,
Tertullian, Origen. Justin First Apology: 30—"What ex-
cludes the supposition that this person whom you call
Christ was a man, of human origin, and did these miracles
you speak of by magic arts, and so appeared to be God's
Son?" [16]
Moreover, after Jesus' death his followers continued to
credit him with magical activities. Many sects in gnostic
Christianity practiced magic and remembered and revered
Jesus as the great magician. The apocryphal gospels add
many magical traits to the picture of Jesus. Whether from
tradition or invention they show that many, perhaps most,
Christians thought of Jesus as doing the things a magician
would do.
"Miracles" (including magical cures and the like), when
they do happen, are usually the results of suggestion (often
hypnotic) and therefore depend both on the practitioner's
"power of suggestion" and the patient's "suggestibility" (for
which the ancient terms were "spirit" and "faith").

Once the social requirements of status and decorum are met, the same man will be called son of a god by his admirers, a magician by his enemies. These terms refer to a single social type, and that type is the one characterized by the actions listed above, which make up by far the greatest part of the Gospels' reports about Jesus.

It is significant that neither Jesus nor his followers denied the charge that he "had" a spirit; on the contrary they admitted it, but claimed the spirit was a holy one (Jn. 1:32 ff; Mk. 1:10). This charge would explain Jesus' recurrent warnings against being "scandalized" at him or being ashamed of him, or denying him before men, which appear in both John and the Synoptics.

After Jesus' death the charge that he had been a magician continued commonly in both Jewish and pagan circles. Justin First Apology 30, Origin, Tertullian, Arnobius, Sanhedrin 43a; 107b and Sotah 47a represent Jesus as a pupil of Rabbi Joshua ben Perahyah who appears in Babylonian magic as a great magician who had ascended into heaven and mastered all the demons.

These accusations were denied but not fundamentally countered by Jesus' followers, of whom some not only admitted but celebrated his achievements as a magician. The question was not his control of spirits but only the means by which he had achieved it.

Both Jews and pagans—who did not become followers of Jesus but admitted his magical powers—attempted to make use of them in their own operations, even in his own lifetime, Mk. 9:38 f. Similar usage continued in Palestine as late as the Second Century (Acts 19:13 ff).

The accounts of Jesus' followers indicate strongly that he practiced and taught magic (Mk. 6:7, 13, 14; Lk. 10:7). After his death they continued and developed these practices (Acts 3:6; 5:5, 9, 15f; 13:9ff; 14:8ff; Mk. 11:13ff, 20ff; Lk. 9:54).

Paul is credited with miraculously effective curses, a hallmark of the magician. Paul wrote that he had "handed over to Satan for destruction of the flesh" a libertine member of the Corinthian church (I Cor. 5:3 ff). This may in part account for Paul's claim to have some strange power over his congregations (I Cor. 4:19; 5:3; II Cor. 6:7; 10:13; 12:19–13:7). The widespread practice of magic in gnostic Christianity is notorious (Irenaeus, Hippolytus). It may be that the gnostic wing was larger than that which subsequently became "orthodox."

Far more important was the essentially magical nature of the fundamental rites of initiation (baptism) and communion (eucharist) by which practically all the Christian communities were constituted and held together. The magical character of baptism is made particularly clear by Paul (I Cor. 15:29): "Those who are baptized on behalf of the dead" to prove that the dead must be raised.

Baptism and eucharist testifies that this sort of thought was not secondary in Christianity, but primitive. The same follows from Paul's account of Christianity as essentially salvation by possession—by the practice of "speaking with tongues." As I Cor. 12 makes clear, this was the utterance incomprehensible sounds, thought by the believers to be the speech of the spirit which possessed the speakers, a common symptom of schizophrenia.[17] It was so common at Corinth that it disrupted worship. Paul insisted it is not the greatest gift of the spirit. The spirit also gives wisdom, knowledge, faith, the ability to perform cures, do miracles, prophesy, distinguish good from evil spirits, and interpret things spoken in "tongues." This does not reduce the importance of magic in Paul's view. On the contrary, it extends it to the whole of normal as well as abnormal psychology.

The spirit speaking in jabberwocky is a characteristic form of magical utterance. There are magical words with secret significance, but most are apparently meaningless combinations of letters. It shows that the spirit is in him and acting through him. The spirit which spoke through Christians and the spirit which spoke through the pagan magician spoke the same characteristic language.

This was already recognized in antiquity and its recognition resulted in many of the persecutions which Christianity everywhere called forth. These persecutions require explanations both because of their frequency and because of the general tolerance throughout the Roman empire for cults of oriental gods and deified men. The consistent opposition to Christianity evidently resulted from something characteristic of the new religion. What was it?

The common answer is the Christians' refusal to worship other gods. But other worshippers of Yahweh—the Jews and the Samaritans—also refused to worship other gods and they were not generally persecuted. Consequently the Christians had to explain the persecutions as inspired either by the demons or by the Jews, who, they said, denounced them to the authorities (Acts 13:50; 14:2; 17:6, 13; 18:12; etc., I Thess. 2:15; Apoc. 2:9). But what for? Certainly not for refusing to worship other gods, which was the basis of the Jewish faith. For political conspiracy? But there is no evidence that Christians were, generally, subversive in politics—at least after the year 70 A.D. [18]—and they were not generally accused of plotting political revolution. What they were accused of was the practice of magic and other crimes associated with magic: human sacrifice, cannibalism, and incest.

Magic figures conspicuously in charges against Christians from the Second Century on (Origen). Moreover the Christians made considerable use of this charge against each other (Irenaeus, Hippolytus and Epiphanius). Magic has been commonly neglected in discussions of the persecutions. The apologists chose to defend Christianity from charges of which most Christians were not guilty; magic would have been an embarrassing topic, therefore they do not mention it, and in refuting the charge of cannibalism they are careful to avoid the question of what actually happens in the eucharist. The acts of the martyrs are propaganda pieces, mostly intended to represent the Christians as innocent victims martyred solely because of monotheism; therefore they usually say nothing of any of the *flagitia cohaerentia nomini* (Pliny, Epistulae X. 96.2). History should not use such material uncritically.

Recapitulation and Conclusions

1) The fact that Jesus is not represented as a magician by the Gospels is insignificant; "magician" was a dirty word. The significant fact is that he is represented as the possessor of the holy spirit and as "the Son of God," a supernatural being recognized by demons as able to command them; he is represented as a successful magician would have represented himself.

2) That Jesus does not use long spells or magic rites is insignificant. Once a magician "had" his spirit, he need only command and it would instantly obey. Here too, the Gospels represent Jesus as a successful magician would have represented himself.

3) The miracle stories are shot through with minor traits of magical practice.

4) The Gospels' stories generally are stories of things magicians claimed to do, and they add up to an account of a magician's life. Jesus' career began when he was possessed by a spirit which drove him into the wilderness. After surviving the ordeals to which the spirits there subjected him he returned to Galilee, where he made his reputation as an exorcist and miracle worker and developed it by cures of magical traits. He then empowered his disciples to exorcize

121

and perform similar cures (Mk. 6:7-13). His fame thus became so great that magicians outside the circle of his followers began to use his name in their exorcisms (Mk. 9:38 f). He introduced a secret meal in which his followers were united with him by being given bread and wine which were declared to be his flesh and blood (Mk. 14:17-25). In all these respects his work can be paralleled from the claims and careers of other magicians. The career most fully reported is that of Apollonius of Tyana, but if the facts were known a closer parallel would perhaps be found in that of Jesus' contemporary Simon, the Samaritan magician, who also did miracles, claimed to be a power come down from heaven, and was credited with the introduction of mystery rites (Acts 8:9ff; Irenaeus).[19]

Finally Jesus claimed to be the Messiah and, somehow, to be able to admit his followers to the kingdom of God, and this claim resulted in his execution by the Romans. In these respects too, his career has magical parallels. Josephus reports that in Palestine at this period there was a plague of messianic magicians who similarly raised men's hopes for the coming of the kingdom, and who come to similarly bad ends at the hands of the Romans (BJ II. 258ff; AJ XX. 97, 188).[20]

The hypothesis that Jesus practiced magic helps to explain some of the major problems raised by the Gospels' account of his career. Jesus claimed to be the Messiah and bringer of the kingdom of God. But there is no clear indication of his functional relation to the kingdom as already present. This is the more surprising because even in the sketchy stories given by Josephus about the other messianic magicians, their functions in relation to the kingdom are clear—they will use their magical powers to protect their followers and overthrow the Romans. So, too, the functional relation of the Baptist to the kingdom he foretold was clear. So the silence of the Gospels on Jesus' functional relation to the kingdom is amazing. It requires an explanation.

A considerable number of Jesus' sayings imply that not only he, but also some of his disciples, are already in the kingdom. In addition, there is a definite, practical way to get in. That the mystery of the kingdom *has been given* to the disciples (Mk. 4:11) suggests that there was some initiatory rite. Some evidence indicates that this rite was a baptism which Jesus administered secretly to a chosen few of his followers. Lk. 7:28 fits with Jn. 3:3 ff—none born of women is greater than the Baptist, but the least in the kingdom is greater than he. What then, was the least in the kingdom born of? John answers of water and the spirit (as opposed to those born of flesh) for only those born of water and spirit can enter the kingdom. "Of water and spirit" is evidently a reference to Jesus' baptism which gave the spirit as opposed to the Baptist's which did not.

How did Jesus' baptism admit his followers to the kingdom? There is reason to believe that there was in Palestine in Jesus' time a magical technique for ascending and causing others to ascend into the heavens. If Jesus practiced such a technique it would explain the statement that "the Law and the prophets were in force until John the Baptist; since then the good news about the kingdom of God has been proclaimed and anyone can force his way into it" (Lk. 16:16; Mt. 11:12). In the magical techniques of ascent to the heavens the magician must overcome the resistance of the demonic or angelic guards who bar the way. These powers Jesus has overcome (Col. 2:9 ff).

It was while performing such a baptism that Jesus was arrested. The rite was secret. He chose a lonely garden, and went there late at night, after the ceremony of the eucharist had assured the magical union of his circle of initiates. Since he did not wish to be interrupted (this is essential in magic) he set guards (Mk. 14:32-34). He had no intention of being arrested if he could help it. The agony, therefore, has no likelihood, and it was witnessed by no one. When the guards fell asleep and the police arrived unexpectedly they surprised both Jesus and the initiate (Mk. 14:51), the robe was seized and the youth fled naked, the proper magical costume in the proper magical setting. If this was not an initiation, what was the young man doing with Jesus at such an hour, in such a place, and in such a costume?

When one has travelled this far with Smith's work there is a sense of silence. A great boundary has been crossed and it requires time to catch one's breath and survey the landscape. As with all great moments it is time to realize that everything has changed. Our vision has permanently altered, our point of view is no longer what it was.

The author has many more very significant items to communicate and the interested reader must consult his book to get the very important documentation which he brings to the Secret Gospel of Mark.

At this point I shall cease my attempt to summarize the body of the author's work. He continues to demonstrate that the Pauline concept of baptism, conceived as a means of ascent to the heavens (the resurrection rite), was derived from Jesus, and this was presumably a vivid hypnotic experience of ascent. The rite liberated its recipient from the Mosaic law. The many contradictory passages of the Gospels are explained as those relating to the public ministry as opposed to the esoteric doctrines given to the initiate.

The notion grew that Jesus' baptismal practice gave the spirit which the Baptist's did not. Further, the baptism encouraged the libertine tradition in early Christianity since those who have entered the kingdom are free of the law.

The survival of the Christian sect makes the disappearance of all works of its founders a noteworthy problem. That they were all illiterate is improbable. The libertine consequences of Jesus' baptismal practice probably helped

James and his party to get rid of both the apostles and their writings. What early Christianity was like can be inferred from the things Paul opposed. Paul, however, had substantially preserved the teachings of Jesus' baptism, hence the disappearance of Paul's baptismal teaching from the works of second century Christian writers.

Smith then examines the evidence concerning the libertine sect of Carpocrates which so concerned Clement, particularly the ritual copulation in agapai which turned on the saying "give to him who asketh of thee." He concludes that the Carpocratians derive from and continued the primitive libertine Christian tradition.

The question assails the reader: Is it possible? So many contradictions in the Gospels seem to fall into place, so many puzzles and mysteries seem less puzzling and mysterious. The esoteric doctrines of the kingdom of God and the freedom from Mosaic law (if they were teachings for the initiated) and the parables and strict injunctions to preserve the Mosaic law (if this was the exoteric teaching for the public) the contradictions and strangeness of the Gospels begin to evaporate and a corner of the curtain is lifted on the darkest mystery of history.

One is assailed by doubts that perhaps we are reading too much into the fragment of the longer text of Mark. Yet the evidence gleaned from non-Christian sources, the horror which early Christian practices evoked, the evidence of the early Christian writers, as well as the gnostic rivals of what became orthodox Christianity all present evidence that demands to be heard. Points otherwise incompatible become intelligible and provide confirmation of the interpretation submitted by Smith.

Footnotes

1. See Moses Hadas and Morton Smith, *Heroes and Gods* (New York: Harper & Row, 1965), xiii.
2. London: Hodder & Stoughton, 1970.
3. Ibid. xviii-xix.
4. Ibid. xiv.
5. Ibid. xviii.
6. J.M. Allegro, *The Dead Sea Scrolls* (Middlesex: Penguin Books Ltd. 1956).
7. *The Sacred Mushroom and the Cross*, op cit. xviii.
8. Ibid. xvi
9. Leo W. Schwarz, *Wolfson of Harvard* (Philadelphia: The Jewish Publication Society of American, 1978), xxxiii.
10. S.G.F. Brandon, *The Judgment of the Dead* (New York: Charles Scribner's Sons, 1967), p. 106.
11. Les Religions Orientales dans le Paganisme Romain-Paris, 1929, p. 281. In general see *The Jewish Encyclopedia* Vol. VIII, p. 255 (Funk and Wagnalls Company, New York: 1904).
12. Morton Smith, *Jesus the Magician* (New York: Harper & Row, 1978), p. 192.

13. Morton Smith, *Clement of Alexandria and a Secret Gospel of Mark* (Cambridge: Harvard University Press, 1973), p. 222.

14. Those who wish to pursue this study further should consult Morton Smith's *Jesus the Magician* which extends and to some degree corrects the earlier work on which much of this essay is based.

15. Franz Cumont, *The Mysteries of Mithra* (New York: Dover Publications, Inc. 1956), p. 105, 107-8.

16. *Early Christian Fathers,* ed. Cyril C. Richardson, tr. E.R. Hardy (New York: The Macmillan Company, 1970), p. 260.

17. See, e.g., Sigmund Freud, Standard Edition Vol. XIV p. 196-199 (London: The Hogarth Press, 1957).

18. Cf. S.G.F. Brandon, *The Fall of Jerusalem and the Christian Church* (London: S.P.C.K. 1974), Ch. VI, where evidence pointing to the existence of a political element in the original Christian movement is examined. See also the Slavonic version of Josephus' *Wars* which indicates that Josephus regarded Christianity as primarily a revolutionary movement against Roman rule in Palestine. See Edwin Hatch, *The Influence of Greek Ideas on Christianity* (New York: Harper & Brothers, 1957), p. 293, citing Origen: *Contra Celsus.*

19. See Moses Hadas and Morton Smith, *Heroes and Gods* op. cit., Ch. XV, "A Summary of 'The Life of Appolonius of Tyana' by Philostratus."

20. See James Parkes, *The Conflict of the Church and the Synagogue* (Cleveland and New York: The World Publishing Company, 1961), p. 22: "[Conflicts] were precipitated by the flood of Messiahs who sprang up in the first half of the first Century A.D. According to the calendar in use among the Jews at that time, the coming of the Messianic age was expected about the middle of the First Century."

II
"The Sacred Mushroom and the Cross"
BY JOHN ALLEGRO

As previously noted, John Allegro has devoted himself to a study of philology. "Our fresh doubts about the historicity of Jesus and his friends stem not from new discoveries about the land and people of Palestine of the First Century, but about the nature and origin of the languages they spoke and the origins of their religious cults." [1]

In the case of Christianity the historical questions are perhaps more acute.[2] The Church destroyed everything it considered heretical, and what we know of such movements derives largely from the refutations by the early Fathers of their beliefs. But at least we no longer have to squeeze such "aberrations" into a century or two after 30 A.D. "Christianity" under its various names had been thriving for centuries before that. As we may now appreciate, it was the more original cult that was driven underground by the combined efforts of the Roman, Jewish, and ecclesiastical authorities; it was the supreme "heresy" which came on, made terms with the secular powers, and became the Church of today.

The fungus recognized today as the *Amanita Muscaria*, or

Fly-Agaric, has been known from the beginning of history.[3] Beneath the skin of its characteristic red-and-white spotted cap, there is concealed a powerful hallucinatory poison. Its religious use among certain Siberian peoples and others has been the subject of study in recent years, and its exhilarating and depressive effects have been clinically examined.[4] These include the stimulation of the perceptive faculties so that the subject sees objects much greater or much smaller than they really are, colors and sounds are much enhanced, and there is a general sense of power, both physical and mental, quite outside the normal range of human experience.

For those contemplating the study of this exotic subject, it should be borne in mind that while most of the toxic species are not fatal to man, a small number of mushrooms have toxins that are fatally poisonous while others affect the central nervous system and are very debilitating. It should be carefully noted that very few of the total number of mushrooms have been tested, and the pharmacopoeia of the medical profession is often helpless to alleviate the alarming symptoms that may unfortunately present itself. Field work and study should be carried on only in the presence of botanists who are authorities on the fungi.

The mushroom has always been a thing of mystery—it was, in fact, God himself, manifest on earth. To the mystic it was the divinely given means of entering heaven. To pluck such a precious herb was attended at every point with peril. Some form of substitution was necessary to make an atonement to the earth robbed of her offspring. Yet such was the divine nature of the Holy Plant, as it was called, that only the god could make the necessary sacrifice. To redeem the Son, the Father had to supply even the "price of redemption." These are all phrases used of the sacred mushroom, as they are of the Jesus of Christian theology.

Only when we can discover the nomenclature of the sacred fungus within and without the cult can we begin to understand its function and theology. Many of the most secret names of the mushroom go back to ancient Sumerian, the oldest written language known to us. It now appears that this ancient tongue provides a bridge between the Indo-European languages and the Semitic group which includes the languages of the Old Testament. Even languages so apparently different as Greek and Hebrew, when they can be shown to derive from a common font, point to a communality of culture at some early stage.[5]

In biblical studies, the old divisions between Old and New Testament areas of research, never very meaningful except to the Christian theologian, become even less valid. As far as the origins of Christianity are concerned, we must look not to just intertestamental literature, the Apocrypha and Pseudo epigrapha, and the newly discovered writings from the Dead Sea, nor even merely to the Old Testament and other Semitic works, but we have to bring into consideration Sumerian religions and mythological texts and the classical writings of Asia Minor, Greece and Rome. The Christian Easter is as firmly linked to the Bacchic Anthesteria as the Jewish Passover.

The viciousness which characterized the Zealots and made them feared and hated probably owed much to the stimulation of the drugs they obtained from the cap of their sacred fungus. In association with the Zealots, Josephus later names the Sicarii, "Assassins," who created so much havoc during the revolt of 66-73. A.D. The name of Sicarii is usually assumed to be a reference to the short sickle-shaped blade (Latin *sica*) carried by the Assassins under their cloaks.

We may now more probably derive the name Sicarii from another name for the fungus. It has come down into modern Persian in *saqratiyun*, "mushroom," but it is more generally known in the form it assumes in the New Testament mythology, as the name of Jesus' betrayer "Iscariot." Thanks to our recent researches, it is now possible to break through the "cover story" of the Gospels and Acts and penetrate to the very much more significant level of meaning beneath. For the whole of the Jesus story is quite fictional. It was widely disseminated for the dual purpose of conveying to the scattered members of the cult special, secret names of the sacred fungus, concealed in such nicknames as "Iscariot" and "Boanerges," and for laying a smoke screen to deceive the authorities about the organization's subversive activities. Despite the incredibly favorable attitude displayed in the New Testament toward the hated Romans, it does not seem to have allayed the suspicion of local governors, who were instructed to seek out participants in the mystic Christian rites, torture them to discover their secrets, and then execute them by the vilest and most painful means. Contemporary Roman historians can hardly find words base enough to describe these worshipers of the "Chrestus."

We may also recognize today that the Gospel stories were no more successful in deceiving the Jewish authorities. Here and there in Jewish literature appear previously incomprehensible epithets applied to Jesus which relate to the sacred mushroom. Most rabbinic traditions about the Christian hero have been obliterated by the church censors, through whose hands almost all such records have come down to us. Where, as in such cases, stories and epithets have been allowed to stand uncorrected, it is usually because the censors failed to understand their significance, and even Jews had long ago ceased to understand their original meaning, or had deemed it wiser to banish such traditions from their minds for fear of further persecution by the now dominant church.

It would seem, then, that the "Zealots" and the "Sicarii" are one and the same, and that early Christianity was closely connected with this revolutionary movement. For, as we can now recognize for the first time, the old mushroom cult was indeed at the very heart of ancient Yahwism. Its essence was fertility worship, whose manifestations in popular sexual cult practices prophetic reformations were forever trying to eradicate. Now that we can decipher the old Hebrew names of the gods and heroes, we can understand their fertility and mushroom significance, and thus recover just those elements of old Israelitism that the post-exilic religionists did their best to forget. Clearly, the old fungus cult was not so easily suppressed, but continued underground as a mystery religion transmitted secretly between initiates sworn to silence about the central features of their faith. Thus Essenism and Christianity could claim to represent the True Israel, and, with some justification, accuse "Orthodox" Judaism of having departed from authentic Yahwism. In the same way, the Christian "heresies," which caused the established Church so much trouble in the early centuries, with some justice maintained that they were the divinely appointed recipients of the occult knowledge of God, and that the institution which was so intent on hounding them out of existence had lost, or never had, "the mysteries of Christ."

It is furthermore now plain that the cult of the sacred fungus was not confined to old Israelitism and its latter-day manifestations; it lies at the heart of many of the Asian mystery cults, such as the Bacchic worship. The ground was already prepared, therefore, for Jewish-Christian cells to flourish in Asia Minor and the larger cities of the empire, and thus to provide a network of communication throughout the Mediterranean lands for the passing of information between dissident groups. A significant feature of such closely knit religious communities as the Essenes and Christians was the way members could pass freely between groups, with a minimum of money and luggage, always certain of hospitality and the free provision of the necessities of life and travel. It is small wonder that such societies were always the objects of great suspicion by the Romans, who rightly recognized that through their channels of information rebellions could flare up simultaneously in widely separated centers throughout the empire.[6]

Those mushroom epithets and holy invocations that the Christian cryptographers wove into their stories of the man Jesus and his companions can now be recognized, and the main features of the Christian cult laid bare. The sparse references to one "Christus" or "Chrestus" in the works of contemporary non-Christian historians tell us nothing about the nature of the man, and only very dubiously do they support his historicity. They simply bear witness to the fact, never in dispute, that the stories of the Gospels were in circulation soon after 70 A.D.

The Aramaic translations of Greek names used in the New Testament provide problems since it is difficult to see how the translations fit the names; "Boanerges" to mean "Sons of Thunder"[7] or Barnabas "Son of Consolation." Yet these aberrations of proper names and their pseudo-translations are of crucial importance. They provide us with a clue as to the nature of original Christianity. Concealed within are secret names for the sacred fungus, the sect's "Christ." The deliberately deceptive nature of their mis-translations puts the lie to the whole of the "cover-story" of the man Jesus and his activities. Once the ruse is penetrated, then research can go ahead fast with fitting the Christian phenomenon more firmly into the cultic patterns of the ancient Near East. Many apparently unrelated facts about the ubiquitous mystery cults of the area and their related mythologies suddenly begin to come together into an intellectually satisfying whole.

The Sumerian name for Apollo is *Paian* from which derives the Greek plant name *Paionia*, our Paeony. Both go back to an original BAR-IA-U-NA which reappears with only the *a* and *u* combined in the New Testament *Barionas,* "Bar-Jona," Peter's surname. The Sumerian BAR-IA-U-NA means "capsule of fecundity; womb," and we can connect it with a number of other mushroom names relating to the little "womb" or vulva from which the stem of the fungus emerges.

The device used so often in the New Testament is of following a genuine name for the sacred fungus with a false translation for the sake of the plot—an established part of mushroom mythology as the writer of Mark's Gospel "explained" Boanerges as "Sons of Thunder."

The "stumbling-block" figure occurs frequently in the New Testament, but of particular note is its application to the apostle Peter following Jesus' prophecy of his forthcoming suffering, "Peter took him and began to rebuke him saying, 'God forbid, Lord! This shall never happen to you.' But he turned and said to Peter 'Get behind me, Satan! You are a stumbling block to me'" (Mt. 16:22f).

Peter's name is a play on the Semitic *pitra,* "mushroom" and his patronymic, Bar-jonah, is really a fungus name cognate with Paeonia, the Holy Plant. Now called a "stumbling-block," he is given the *tiqla,* "bolt-mushroom" name, a theme which is repeated elsewhere in that over-emphasized and completely misunderstood passage about having the keys of the kingdom.

"And I tell you, you are Peter,[8] and on this rock I will build my church, and the gates of Hades shall not prevail against it. I will give you the keys of the kingdom of heaven" (Mt. 16:18 f).

The sacred fungus was the "bolt" or "key" that gave access to heaven and to hell, a double reference to the shape as a knobbed bolt for opening doors, and to its ability to open the way to new and exciting mystical experiences.

Calling the apostle "Satan" is in line with his other title

Cephas. Both names are in fact plays on designations of the mushroom of that other "bulb" plant, the onion. Greek and Latin apply the name *setanion, setania* to the onion, and Latin has *caepa, cepa* for that vegetable cognate with the French cepe, ceps, "mushroom."

The well-known word-play in Mt. 16:18, "You are Peter (Petros) and upon this rock (petra) I shall build my church," can now be seen as of much greater relevance to the cult than a mere pun on Peter's title, Cephas, and the Aramaic word for "stone," *Kepha.* The real point of the whole passage is the word-play on the names of the sacred fungus that "Peter" represented.

The commission of authority: "I will give you the keys of the kingdom of heaven, and whatever you bind on earth shall be bound in heaven, and whatever you loose on earth shall be loosed in heaven" (Mt. 16:19), has its verbal basis in an important Sumerian mushroom name, MACH-BA(LA)-ANTA-TAB-BA-RI, read as "though art the permitter (releaser) of the kingdom" by a play on three or four Aramaic words spun out of the Sumerian title. It has, probably, like most of the directives and homilies of the "cover" story, no real-life significance. Least of all would the passage have been taken by the cult members that one of their number should take upon himself the kind of spiritual authority indicated by the face reading of the text. The sole prerogative of "binding" and "loosing" lay with God. To the worshipper of the sacred fungus, the deity was present in the mushroom and offered his servants the "key" to a new and wonderful mystic experience. It was this "re-birth," as it was called, that cleared away the debts of the past and gave promise of a future free from the cultic "sin" that destroyed the initiates' free communion with God.

It was left to a later development of the cult, also calling themselves "Christians" and reading the words at their face value, to accord to their leader and his designates a divine authority for forgiving sins and pronouncing on moral matters which Judaism would have found abhorrent, even blasphemous.

As for Barnabas, "Son of Consolation," the consonant group n-b-s- derived from the Accadian NABASU, "red dyed wool," and in Aramaic *nabusa* is the name of a certain red wooly caterpillar that infects the pear, or Service tree. The motif of "red flecked with white" continues in the Greek and Latin names of the "giraffe," *nabus* a ruddy color picked out with white spots—a good description of the *Aminita muscaria* coloration. It is the same n-b-s- verbal group that is the significant part of the new Testament character, "Joseph, called Barnabas."

"Joseph who was surnamed by the apostles Barnabas (which means Son of Encouragement), a Levite, a native of Cyprus, sold a field which belonged to him and brought the money and laid it at the apostles' feet" (Acts 4:32-37).

The surname of this philanthropist has caused the commentators much trouble in the past, for the New Testament cryptographer has given us another false translation, telling us that "Barnabas" means "Son of Encouragement." He implies that the first part "Bar" is the Aramaic "son of" and the *nabas* at the end represents another Semitic word meaning "Encouragement." In point of fact there is no extant root which offers that meaning (*ahmats* Heb.). The name is not, indeed, Aramaic at all: the first element is the Sumerian BAR, "skin" and the second is our "giraffe," *nabus,* or "red dyed wool," *nabasu,* "red-with-white-spots," being yet another epithet of the *Amenita muscaria.*

The name "Boanerges" has given scholars a difficult problem. It has been assumed to be Aramaic, a kind of semi-jocular nickname applied to the fiery-tempered brothers, James and John, by Jesus in the colloquial tongue of Palestine of the first century, but which is incomprehensible in any known Aramaic dialect. The text adds the "explanation" of the name as "Sons of Thunder" (Mk. 3:17). It has been assumed that the reference is to the brothers' suggestion that they call fire down upon the Samaritan village that would not receive the Master and his friends (Lk. 9:54). The trouble is that "Boanerges" does not mean "Sons of Thunder." For one thing the first part "Boane" is not the Semitic *bne,* "sons of," even though it sounds something like it; for another, the remaining part, *-rges,* does not mean "thunder" (the Aramaic would connote agitation, while the Hebrew, anger). Nevertheless, the phrase has an air of authenticity which would deceive the cursory reader, and this was certainly its intention. The whole Sumerian phrase from which the Greek nickname comes was GEShPU-An-Ur (read as *pu-an-ur-ges)* meaning "mightly man (holding up) the arch of heaven," a fanciful image of the stem supporting the canopy of the mushroom, seen in cosmographical terms a view of the universe which saw heaven and earth as born from the vulva of some vast primeval fungus.

We have too readily assumed, in seeking an explanation for the strange incompatibility between "Boanerges" and its "translation," that the text was defective, that later scribes being unfamiliar with Aramaic had miswritten the nickname. Now, thanks to our present discoveries, we are able to take a more appreciative view of the craft of the New Testament cryptographer. Neither he nor his copyists had made a mistake: we had, in taking the text at its face value. The name was not a jocular expression given by an Aramaic-speaking rabbi to two of his friends. It is not, as we now realize, Aramaic. The clue to its mushroom affinities has lain all along in the "translation" which, as such, is of course quite spurious. But "sons of thunder" *is* a well-known name for the fungus found elsewhere in Semitic texts, and supported by the old Greek name *keraunion,* "thunder-fungus," after *keraunos,* "thunder." The reference is to the belief that mushrooms were born of thunder, the voice of the god in the storm, since it was noticed that they appeared in the ground after rainstorms.

It is a particularly clear example of a number of such instances in the text of the New Testament where a genuine mushroom name is followed by a spurious translation for the sake of the plot of the story. As here, the false renderings have usually some particular relevance for the sacred fungus even though they do not interpret, as they affirm, the accompanying foreign word.

What they do indicate very clearly is the unreal nature of the whole surface story of the Gospels and Acts. Put very simply, if the writer has gone to the trouble purposefully to conceal his secret name for the mushroom by giving it a misleading rendering, near enough in this case to deceive the cursory reader, then it follows that behind the story of Jesus and his companions there lies a secret layer of meaning which was not intended to be read or understood by the outsider. Since mushrooms nowhere appear in the surface story, and yet are clearly involved in the cryptic names, it must mean that the secret level of understanding is the significant one for the intended reader as for the cryptographer; what appears on the surface is unreal and never expected to be taken seriously by those within the cult. There is no escape from this dilemma: if our new understanding of "Boanerges" is correct, the historicity and validity of the New Testament story is in ruins. A subterfuge of this nature, bearing as it does on what we now see was a widespread and very ancient mushroom cult, can only mean that the "real" Christianity was heavily involved with it; in which case the story of Jesus was a hoax for the benefit of the Jewish and Roman authorities engaged in persecuting the cult.

If we need radically to reassess the Old Testament traditions in the light of the new discoveries,[9] the New Testament situation is far more bleak as far as the Christian is concerned. We must be in no doubt of the effect that importing a new mushroom element into the New Testament picture must have on our understanding of the origin and nature of Christianity. It needed only the decipherment of one of the strange non-Greek phrases in such terms to upset the whole previous picture of the beginning and growth of the church. If, for instance, "Boanerges" is correctly to be explained as a name of the sacred fungus, and the impossible "translation" appended in the text, "Sons of Thunder," is equally relevant to the mushroom, then the validity of the whole New Testament story is immediately undermined. For the pseudo-translation demonstrates an intention of deceit, and since mushrooms appear nowhere in the "surface" tale of Jesus, it follows that the secret references to the cult must be the true relevance of the whole. If the writers have gone to the trouble of concealing by ingenious literary devices, here, and as we have seen, in many cases elsewhere, secret names of the mushroom, not only must its worship have been central to the religion, but the exigencies of the time must have demanded they should be transmitted among the initiates and their successors in a way that would not bring their enemies down upon them. It therefore follows that the "surface" details of the story, names, places, and possibly doctrinal teachings must be equally as false as the pseudo-rendering of the secret names.

Plant mythology provided the New Testament cryptographer with their cover. The Christians believed that they were the true spiritual heirs to ancient Israel. So it was an obvious device to convey to the scattered cells of the cult reminders of their most sacred doctrines and incantatory names and expressions concealed within a story of a "second Moses," another Lawgiver named after the patriarch's successor in office, Joshua (Gk. Iesous). Thus was born the Gospel myth of the New Testament. How far it succeeded in deceiving the authorities, Jewish and Roman, is doubtful. Certainly the Roman records speak with loathing of the Christians and they were hounded with an extreme ferocity reserved for political troublemakers within the realm. Those most deceived appear to have been the sect which took over the name "Christian" and who formed the basis of the Church.

In the New Testament writings word-play can be a purposeful disguise, a means whereby special secret names of the Holy Plant could be conveyed to the initiate through his informed group-leader without their being revealed to the outsider.

In general there are at least three levels of understanding involved in the New Testament writings. On the surface, there are the Greek words in their plain meaning. How much reality there is at this level is a matter for further inquiry, but probably very little.

Beneath the Greek there lies a Semitic level of understanding (not actual Semitic versions of the Greek texts). It is mainly in this level that the word plays are made.

Under that again there lie the basic conceptions of the mushroom cult. Here is the real stuff of the mystery-fertility philosophy. The passage that likens the Kingdom to a mustard seed, for example, and then speaks of birds nesting in the branches of the grown plant (Mt. 13:31 f), has driven the biblical naturalists to distraction. They could have saved themselves the trouble since the reference, at the "lower" level, is simply a play on the Semitic *Khardela*, "mustard" and *ardila*, "mushroom." Furthermore, the whole discussion about the Kingdom stems from the Semitic root d-b-r, "guide, manage, control," the real meaning of this mystic "Kingdom" into which the initiates into the mysteries hoped to pass.

We should not be tempted to underestimate either the intelligence of those participating in the cult, or their literary methods in committing their vital secrets to written form. In view of the hostility understandably being shown them by the authorities of the time, Roman and Jewish, writing the New Testament at all was scarcely less dangerous than chewing the sacred mushroom.

One explanation for the creation of the mushroom without apparent seed was that the "womb" had been fertilized by thunder, the fungi commonly observed having appeared after thunderstorms. It was thus uniquely begotten. The normal process of fructification had been by-passed. The seed had not fallen from some previous plant, to be nurtured by the earth until in turn it produced a root and stalk. The god had "spoken" and his creative "word" had been carried to earth by the storm-wind, angelic messenger of heaven, and been implanted directly into the vulva. The baby that resulted from this divine union was thus the "Son of God," more truly representative of its heavenly father than any other form of plant or animal life. Here, in the tiny mushroom, was God manifest, the "Jesus" born of the Virgin, "the image of the invisible God, the first-born of all creation . . . in him all the fulness of God was pleased to dwell. . ." (Col. 1:15 ff.).

In the phallic mushroom, the "man-child" born of the "Virgin" womb, we have the reality behind the Christ figure of the New Testament story. In a sense he is representative also of the initiates of the cult, "Christians," or "smeared with semen," as the name means. By imitating the mushroom, as well as by eating it and sucking its juice, or "blood," the Christian was taking into himself the panoply of his god, as the priests in the sanctuary also anointed themselves with the god's spermatozoa found in the juices and resins of special plants and trees. As the priests "served" the god in the temple, the symbolic womb of divine creation, so the Christians and their cultic associates worshipped their god and mystically involved themselves in the creative process. In the language of the mystery cults they sought to be "born again," when, purged afresh of past sin, they could apprehend the god in a drug-induced ecstasy.

The fundamental principle of fertility philosophy was that of balance. To take any of the fruits of the earth necessitated some measure of compensation or sacrifice to the god. To be effective this return payment should be at least qualitatively equivalent to the gift received, so that only the best of the harvest, the first-reaped of the corn and the first-born of the animals, was suitable. In the case of an especially powerful plant like the sacred mushroom, an atoning substitution posed special problems. Since the fungus was the god himself made manifest on earth, no atoning sacrifice by mortals could suffice. The seeker could only bring with him the Holy Plant itself or some symbol of it. In other words, only the god can atone for himself, and herein lies the basis of the Christian doctrine of the Incarnation and Atonement. II Cor. 4:10: "Always carrying in the body the death of Jesus, so that the life of Jesus may be manifested in our bodies."

A great deal of the mythology of the ancient Near East hinges on the theme of the dying and rising god. It is usually seen as symbolism in story form of the process of nature whereby in the heat of summer the earth's greenness disappears in death, to reappear the following spring in new birth. But in the mushroom this is quickened to a matter of days or even hours, the essence of god compressed into the womb and penis of the hermaphrodite mushroom.

One immediate result of the cracking of the already very fragile skin of the New Testament story is that all those doubts about its details which have so exercised scholars over the years are brought sharply back into focus. There always have been extreme difficulties in understanding the story of Jesus. There are in the New Testament picture many kinds of problems posed on historical, geographical, topographical, social, and religious grounds which have never been resolved. But to the Christian scholar they have always seemed of less relevance than the apparently incontrovertible fact of the existence of one semi-divine man who set the whole Christian movement in motion, and without whose existence the inauguration of the Church would seem inexplicable. But if it now transpires that Christianity was only a latter-day manifestation of a religious movement that had been in existence for thousands of years, and in that particular mystery-cult form for centuries before the turn of the era, then the necessity for a founder-figure fades away, and the problems that have for so long beset the exegete become far more urgent. The improbable nature of the tale, quite apart from the "miracle" stories, the extraordinarily liberal attitude of the central figure towards the Jewish "quislings" of the time, his friendly disposition towards the most hated enemies of his people, his equivocation about paying taxes to the Roman government, the howling of Jewish citizens for the blood of one of their own people at the hands of the occupying power, features of the Gospel story which have never rung true, now can be understood for what they have always been: parts of a deliberate attempt to mislead the authorities into whose hands it was known the New Testament documents would fall. The New Testament was a "hoax," but nevertheless a deadly serious and extremely dangerous attempt to transmit to the scattered faithful secrets which the Christians dare not permit to fall into unauthorized hands but to whose preservation they were irrevocably committed by sacred oaths.

Theirs was no gospel to be shouted from the rooftops: Paradise was for none but the favored few. The incantations and rites by which they conjured forth their drug plants, and the details of the bodily and mental preparations undergone before they could ingest their god, were the secrets of the cult to which none but the initiate, bound by fearful oaths, had access.

Very rarely, and then only for urgent practical purposes, were those secrets ever committed to writing. Normally they would be passed from the priest to the initiate by word of mouth; dependent for their accurate transmission on the trained memories of men dedicated to the learning and recitation of their "scriptures." But if, for some drastic reason like the disruption of their cultic centers by war or persecution, it became necessary to write down the precious names of the herbs and the manner of their use and accompanying incantations, it would be in some esoteric form comprehensible only to those within their dispersed communities.

Such an occasion was the Jewish Revolt of 66 A.D. Instigated by members of the cult, swayed by their drug-induced madness to believe God had called them to master the world in his name, they provoked the mighty power of Rome to swift and terrible action. Jerusalem was ravaged, her temple destroyed. Judaism was disrupted and her people driven to seek refuge with communities already established around the Mediterranean coastlands. The mystery cults found themselves without their central fount of authority, with many of their priests killed in the abortive rebellion or driven into the desert. The secrets, if they were not to be lost forever, had to be committed to writing, and yet, if found, the documents must give nothing away or betray those who still dared defy the Roman authorities and continued their religious practices.

The means of conveying the information were at hand, and had from the earliest times contained myths based upon the personification of plants and trees. They were invested with human faculties and qualities and their names and physical characteristics were applied to the heroes and heroines of the stories. Some of these were just tales spun for entertainment, others were political parables, while others were means of remembering and transmitting therapeutic folk-lore. The names of the plants were spun out to make the basis of the stories, whereby the creatures of fantasy were identified, dressed, and made to enact their parts. Here, then was the literary device to spread occult knowledge to the faithful: to tell the story of a rabbi called Jesus, and invest him with the power and names of the magic drug. To have him live before the terrible events that had disrupted their lives, to preach a love between men, extending even to the hated Romans. Thus, reading such a tale, should it fall into Roman hands, even their mortal enemies might be deceived and not probe farther into the activities of the cells of the mystery cults within their territories.

The ruse failed. Christians, hated and despised, were hauled forth and slain by the thousands. The cult well nigh perished. What eventually took its place was a travesty of the real thing, a mockery of the power that could raise men to heaven and give them the glimpse of God for which they gladly died. The story of the rabbi crucified at the instigation of the Jews became an historical peg upon which the new cult's authority was founded. What began as a hoax, became a trap even to those who believed themselves to be the spiritual heirs of the mystery religion and took to themselves the name of "Christian." Above all they forgot, or purged from the cult and their memories, the one supreme secret on which their whole religious and ecstatic experience depended: the names and identity of the source of the drug, the key to heaven—the sacred mushroom.

Let it be repeated: if even only one of the mushroom references of the cryptic phrases of the New Testament were correct, then a new element has to be reckoned with in the nature and origin of the Christian religion. This new element, furthermore, is the key that fits the phenomenon of Christianity firmly into the surrounding mystery cult pattern of the Near East; but it does so at the cost of the validity of the surface story which knows nothing ostensibly of mushroom cults and which offers for its sacred cultic titles and invocations deliberately false "translations." This is not, then, the record of an evangelistic crusade, an open-armed invitation to all men to join a new society of the redeemed, whose sacred meal is no more than a service of remembrance. It is not the manifesto of an organization whose revolutionary tendencies go no further than the exercise of a group communism of property, but whose teaching urges women to submit at all times to their husbands, and slaves to their masters, being "obedient with fear and trembling." It was not for this pacifism that the Romans dragged forth the celebrants of the Christian mysteries and butchered them.

The emphasis in the New Testament teachings about "love" and non-retaliation could, within a small closed society, be practicable. The accounts given by the historians of such in-groups as the Essenes and Therapeutae give that impression of brotherly love and self-control. Even the extraordinary attitude to women and sex and the practice of celibacy which Josephus reports of the Essenes and which became an ideal of the Church might just be feasible in a desert community of ascetics.

Nevertheless, what we learn of the Christians from the Romans who had to live with them, or at least had to try and keep the peace in a racially and religiously fragmented Empire, does little to convince us that the New Testament homiletic teachings were taken seriously by those most immediately concerned. The Roman historian Tacitus, to whom the Christian authorities have looked for the clearest "evidence" of the historicity of Jesus, can hardly find words base enough to use of the sect, "a class hated for their abominations." "A deadly superstition broke out not only in Judea, the first source of the evil, but also in the City (Rome), where all things hideous and shameful from every part of the world meet and become popular. Accordingly, an arrest was made of all who confessed; then, upon their information, an immense multitude was convicted of hatred of the whole human race" *(Odium humani generis).*

Suetonius, to whom reference has also been commonly made to support the historicity of the Gospels, says that around the year 49, "the Jews constantly made disturbances at the instigation of Chrestus" and were expelled from Rome. Whether, even at that early stage, the authorities were being led to believe that Chrestus or Christus was a man and not the source of the "disturbing" drug (Pliny has described those who have anointed [*Khristos*] themselves with the juice of the Mandrake, its properties being so beneficial that it was called Chreston, *Krestos,* Gk. "good, health-bestowing"), we cannot tell from this passage. The Gospels can hardly have been in circulation before 70. A.D. The passing reference does at least witness to the fractious nature of the sect, and to the hostile attitude of Jews in the city on whom this kind of religious fanaticism, claiming for itself a Jewish origin, would inevitably react to their detriment.

Elsewhere Suetonius speaks of Christians as "a class of men given to a new and wicked superstition, and there seem to have been reports circulating that they practiced infanticide, cannibalism and unrest." Garbled reports about the sacred "Christ"-food eaten in a common meal would almost inevitably lead to the idea that the "Christians" were eating human flesh. Indeed, the Catholic worshipper is so assured even today that through the miracle of transubstantiation he is actually eating Christ's flesh and drinking his blood.

If some aspects of the "Christian" ethic still seem worthwhile today, does it add to their authority that they were promulgated two thousand years ago by worshippers of the *Amenita muscaria?*

Footnotes

1. John M. Allegro, "The Sacred Mushroom and the Cross" (London: Hodder and Stoughton, 1970), XVIII-XIX.
2. See e.g., Michael Grant, *Jesus An Historian's Review of the Gospels* (New York: Charles Scribner's Sons, 1977), p. 182. "Although the primary interest of the Gospel writers was spiritual, and history came second, the Christian Church has always from their time onwards been preoccupied, more than any of its rivals, with the idea that Jesus' life *was history:* and with good reason, since Christianity is the only religion which stands or falls by supposed historical happenings."
3. As his source book for the study of mycology Allegro uses John Ramsbottom, *Mushrooms and Toadstools* (London: Collins, 1953). In addition to this excellent study I recommend for American readers Orson K. Miller, Jr., *Mushrooms of North America* (New York: E.P. Dutton & Co., Inc. 1972).
4. Allegro. op. cit., p. XV. See also John M. Allegro, *The*

Chosen People (New York: Doubleday & Co., Inc. 1971), p. 243.

5. See Cyrus H. Gordon, *The Common Background of Greek and Hebrew Civilizations* (New York: W.W. Norton & Co., Inc. 1965); Cyrus H. Gordon, *The Ancient Near East* (New York: W.W. Norton & Co., Inc. 1965); John Phillip Cohane, *The Key* (New York: Schocken Books, 1976).

6. Allegro, *The Chosen People,* op. cit., Ch. 16.

7. See S.G.F. Brandon, *Jesus and the Zealots* (New York: Charles Scribner's Sons, 1967), p. 203, note 6 and references.

8. For some reason unknown to philology the word "peter" in modern American slang is used as a covert reference to the male sex organ. See Lester V. Berry and Melvin Van Den Bark, *The American Thesaurus of Slang* (New York: Thomas Y. Crowell Company, 1942), p. 147.

9. See John M. Allegro, *The Chosen People,* op. cit.

A Horse Named Desire

". . . all the words of this law: it is not a trivial matter for you, for it is your life . . ." (Deut. 32:46, 47)

While the two books "aretalogized" here may be called "post-Christian", reinforcing the "death" or eclipse of God thesis, they by no means deal with the core of the problem of the disappearance of faith since the rise of scientific theory and philosophy in the seventeenth century. It should be at once noted that science, far. from being a body of knowledge, is a method of study, an approach to problem solving.

The view that science takes of religion is that religious explanations of events are contrary to scientific evidence. Laplace replied to Napoleon, "Sire, I have no need of that hypothesis," when the latter objected that there was no mention of God in his account of the origin of the solar system. In our own day Julian Huxley has put the matter thus: "The advance of natural science, logic, and psychology have brought us to a state at which God is no longer a useful hypothesis." [1]

The hypothesis to be preferred, competing factors being equal, is in general the one which explains all the relevant data most simply, i.e., the fewest assumptions and undefined terms, a requirement known as the Principle of Parsimony or Ockham's razor (what can be done with fewer assumptions is done in vain with more, or plurality is not to be assumed without necessity). The Ptolemaic system is capable of explaining all observed astronomic data. When Copernicus put forth his thesis that the earth revolved around the sun, there was no new doctrine achieved, there were no data which it explained more factually than the former hypothesis and many which it did not explain as well. But the Copernican hypothesis reduced the data involved and made the mathematical calculations much simpler. Through one mathematical relation a large number of motions could be explained which before required separate operations of different properties and laws.

What we are discussing here is not the truth or falsity of a proposition as a working hypothesis but its convenience and application to a large mass of scientific data. Let us reverse the situation and go from the scientific data to the observer of such data. An entirely different situation arises. We enter the psychological and philosophical problem upon the very highest level. It is here that Kant proclaimed the revolutionary discovery of his laws of thought as analogous to that achieved by Copernicus. Those familiar with the revolutionary consequences of the Copernican thesis may rightly be puzzled at Kant's use of this example since his aim "may perhaps be described as a Ptolemaic, anthropocentric metaphysics," [2] not at all Copernican which reduced the earth from its former proud position of central pre-eminence. "His revolution, so far as it was one, was anti-Copernican." [3] Reason must be regarded as self-legislative. Objects must be viewed as conforming to human thought, not human thought to the independently real.

151

This difference in viewpoint runs through the entire gamut of philosophy and scientific thought in Germany and distinguishes it sharply from predominantly empirical thought in England and America. The current continental name for Kant's thought is "phenomenology" and "existentialism." There are various schools and branches but all are deeply influenced by the decisive turning point of Kant's metaphysics.

The older science conceived a point as fixed in space which cannot be in motion. The quantum or wave mechanics theorem expresses the relation between the geometrical and the dynamic aspect of things. In the micro-physics of the quanta, the scientist cannot study physical realities without disturbing them. As an analogy to macro-physics, if a medical doctor seeks to measure your body temperature or blood pressure, the very application of the instruments will to an extent distort the result.

Quantum physics, which introduces a minute discontinuity in nature, does not provide an objective description of the external world but a relation between the state of the external world and the state of knowledge of each observer. The observer is able to obtain partial information that is only probable. What used to be called objective reality is now the relation between the observer and the observed. Einstein made his scientific laws dependent on the relative position of the observer.

Myths are not true in the sense in which other information is true. Their function is to express the vicissitudes of the soul and the moral demands it makes by existing in the world. A myth may also conceal from ourselves our lack of understanding. Religion tends to accept stories as truth rather than as working ideas or hypotheses. The stories become the basis of our religion when they are accepted as describing the reality of the universe. Religion is a rationale to control what empirically seems uncontrollable.

The philosophic point of view uses different language but essentially reaffirms the myth. An example is Hegel in the *Philosophy of History:* "Christ has appeared—a Man who is God—God who is Man; and thereby peace and reconciliation have accrued to the world." [4]

Hegel, like Spinoza, believed the Infinite must exist, must manifest itself. The great philosophical importance of Christianity resides in the doctrine of the Incarnation, according to which God became man and suffered as man.

In Greek religion, typically, there was no belief in immortality. Orphism, a form of Dionysiac cult, was founded upon the belief that the soul is eternal in contrast to his body.[5] It was thought that the soul of man had always existed with God. In contrast to the usual Greek joy in the body, Orphism taught that man's body is his defilement. This belief was taken up by Pythagoreans and Platonists, thereby introducing the cult to the educated classes.

The Orphic myth taught that Zeus had a son who came down to this world only to be captured by the forces of this world, the Titans, who devoured him. Athena was able to save his heart, which Zeus ate. Out of this heart Zeus produced a second son who ruled with him. The particles of the first son were struggling to return to their source, divinity. This story means the presence of the son of God in the world. While the world had tried to conquer the Son, it had failed and the son is both here on earth and with God in heaven, struggling to bring us and all things to God. Here were also Attis, Isis and later Mithra. These and many others taught the story of deity imprisoned in material nature and the hope of man in whom a particle of this divinity was present to escape back to God as the son of God had done before—containing all the elements of the sacrament of the Eucharist.

Into this environment Jews out of Palestine settled in the Hellenistic world, particularly in the new city of Alexandria in Egypt founded by Alexander the Great. They had their own courts, their own civic organization and could live by their own laws and customs. They brought their Scriptures and built a Jewish temple. The Bible was translated into Greek.

Philo, a contemporary of Jesus, gives a reflection of the cultured, cosmopolite Hellenistic Jew of the type Paul was to become. As Paul he taught that only by putting off the mortal and material and by putting on immortality could man achieve his proper end. The great inventor of analogies, he reinterpreted the story cycles of the Old Testament to accord with the philosophy of reason and salvation.[6]

Abraham, in leaving Ur of the Chaldees, left his bodily nature and approached God in a series of steps culminating in the vision at Mamre in which God was revealed as the Three who are One. Abraham was united with and became himself, the Logos incarnate, and thereby divine, a savior of all men who came after him. In the case of Isaac, God changes Sarah into a virgin, the universal mother of all. Then God impregnated her, so that her son, Isaac, was the direct son of God, by virgin birth, though attributed to Abraham.

This was the mystic Judaism that led men out of the material and put on the new spiritual life under the leadership of a savior, a divine man, who was born of a virgin and was the incarnation of the Logos. In his own life he had vanquished the flesh so that he was now intercessor and Savior with God.[7]

This was a pregnant Judaism that was about to give birth to the Christianity of the Church Fathers. Christian Jews quickly made Jesus into the Son of God by a virgin, the Logos Incarnate. The Christian version of the myth differs only in the crucifixion, which Paul found the chief "stumbling block" for his converts. It was through Greek tradition as adapted by Greek Jews that Christianity raised Jesus of Nazareth to its heavenly Savior, the Son of God.

Sir James Jeans in *The Mysterious Universe* writes: "Standing on our microscopic fragment of a grain of sand, we attempt to discover the nature and purpose of the universe which surrounds our home in space and time. Our first impression is something akin to terror. We find the universe terrifying because of its inconceivably long vistas of time which dwarf human history to the twinkling of an eye, terrifying because of our extreme loneliness, and because of the material insignificance of our home in space—a millionth part of a grain of sand out of all the sea-sand in the world. But above all else, we find the universe terrifying because it appears indifferent to life like our own; emotion, ambition and achievement, art and religion all seem equally foreign to its plan. Perhaps we ought to say it appears to be actively hostile to life like our own." [8]

Freud writes: "In my *Future of an Illusion* I was concerned much less with the deepest sources of religious feeling than with what the ordinary man understands by his religion. The ordinary man cannot imagine Providence in any other form but that of a greatly exalted father, for only such a one could understand the needs of the sons of men, or be softened by their prayers and placated by the signs of their remorse. The whole thing is so patently infantile, so incongruous with reality, that to one whose attitude to humanity is friendly it is painful to think that the great majority of mortals will never be able to rise above this view of life. It is even more humiliating to discover what a large number of those alive today, who must see that this religion is not tenable, yet try to defend it inch by inch, as if with a series of pitiable rearguard actions." [9]

Aside from its content, this passage is remarkable for the emotionally charged nature of his attitude. Freud's own father proved a disappointment, for he allowed a bully to knock off his hat which he meekly retrieved from the gutter without taking any retaliatory measures. This incident made a deep imprint on the young Freud. His own father was not "greatly exalted" and he evidently had little patience or sympathy for those who were in search of just such a symbolic figure.

Yet how would he deal with the impression "akin to terror" of Sir James Jeans? Here was, not one of Freud's neurotic patients, but President of the Royal Astronomical Society, author of *The Mathematical Theory of Electricity and Magnetism,* which developed the quantum theory and destroyed the nebular hypothesis of Kant and Laplace. His emphasis on the part played by mathematics in science has been termed "scarcely equalled since Pythagoras."

What is this curious paradox of rationality and terror? Descartes in his *Discourse on Method* (1637): "I thence concluded that I was a substance whose whole essence or nature consists only in thinking . . . I, that is to say, the mind by which I am what I am is wholly distinct from the body." Descartes exalts the mind so Man becomes "res cogitans," pure and thinking substance. Spinoza believes in the possibility of attaining freedom from irrational passions by the very act of understanding them.

Plato emphasized reason and mind, but we are apt to forget that Greek philosophy began in religious ecstasy before it was banished from Plato's Academy and Aristotle's Lyceum. The Dionysian and demonic lurk near the surface of Greek consciousness. There is a madness which is a divine gift; the greatest blessings have come to us in madness. For prophecy is a madness, and the prophetess at Delphi and the priestesses at Dodna when out of their senses have conferred great benefits on Hellas, but when in their senses few or none. Is madness superior to reflection, for reflection is only human, but madness springs from the gods (Phaedrus 244)?

Madness is man's desperate attempt to reach transcendence, to rise beyond himself. The Dionysiac frenzy was more than a "return to nature" in reaction to rationalism. Veneration of the sinister, sanctification of the monstrous, is sought in war, violence, destruction.

Plato pictured the body as representing itself in the psyche as a multiplicity of desires. Knowing what we desire is a function of the intellect. In recognizing desire as a psychological experience, Plato made an enormous advance in the history of psychology. In the *Phaedrus,* Plato describes the psyche (with as much or as little justification as Freud) as made of three parts, a charioteer and two horses. The charioteer is reason or intellect, the Orphic fragment of divinity. One horse is "Desire," a collective symbol of the various desires with which man's mind has to struggle. The second horse is the "spirited part" of the psyche where emotion is central. Despite cooperation from the "spirited" horse, the horse named Desire is so unruly that it plunges the entire psyche from heaven into incarnation in a body. The drama is the hope that the charioteer, reason, will regain control so the psyche can return to the upper region. Unity in the composite psyche is a matter of the harmonious coordination of its various parts and the control of desires and emotions by the intelligence. All the parts should work fully and freely together to make a harmonious whole.

The use of medicine and religion should be not only to satisfy physical and spiritual needs but should be motivated as well to integrate individuals and produce a society not frozen into stability, but in equilibrium where scientific change and social mobility are welcomed and encouraged.

Modern medicine is not sufficient as long as it fails to

weigh the interaction of a man's culture with his bodily condition. Illness has meaning that goes beyond the individual pathology and includes society's view of its consequences. At present it creates barriers and deprives the afflicted of the creative employment of his talents. Resentment and distaste assault his self-esteem and may of itself do more damage than that of the course of the pathology itself. A physician of skill and compassion will not only treat the illness, but will mobilize the environmental factors on his behalf and assist him to resume his place of importance in society.

The words "faith" and "miracle" are so powerful among a large segment of our population and held in such contempt by the great majority of the scientifically educated community that a genuine problem in linguistics arises. I quote an episode from the important book by Erwin R. Goodenough, *The Psychology of Religious Experiences:*

"My former colleague, Ralph Linton, told me about a case he knew of a young Negro who came into a hospital in New York begging for help because he had been hexed and would die at noon the next day. Linton tried to convince the doctors that the man would indeed die if they did not find the person who had cast the spell and get him to relieve the man's mind. The doctors, however, merely examined the patient, found him healthy in every way, smiled at one another behind Linton's back, and put the patient to bed as a disturbed man who needed quiet. But, at noon the next day, he died, and an autopsy found nothing wrong. Now, I do not believe that the spell killed him, but I have no doubt that his belief in the power of the spell did so . . ."

"Witch doctors also cure patients, as do practitioners of faith healing. When the psychoanalysts say that they can do nothing for a patient until his 'resistance' breaks down, I suspect that they have only invented a new term for the old phenomenon. They, too, can do their work only in an atmosphere of faith." [10]

Through faith we do control the uncontrollable—some of it. Where there is faith, there is religion—not intellectual assent, but deep emotional acceptance. Those who have "lost their faith" often speak of the loss as though they had lost their sight or hearing, a faculty of some sort that made them able to do things to themselves and for themselves which they cannot now do. They have lost a real potency, a real power of control.

In every field of discourse, including science, certain terms are accepted without definition, without proof, since there are no intelligible alternatives within that same realm. Because the terms cannot be proved does not indicate an inferior body of knowledge; since postulates are among our least debatable propositions, and we are required by the sheer necessity of being to act upon them as if they were proved, long before we can formulate their logical meaning. Laws, such as the Newtonian laws of motion, refer to abstractions such as mass, points and force that cannot be observed. No experiment could possibly prove them. They are devices for ordering the physical world, an essential part of the language of the concepts of daily life. We are not dealing with fixed bodies and measurements but with events and their functions.

The efficacy of the practice of medicine depends largely on the capacity to arouse the patient's hopes for cure. The successful use of placebos—that is, pharmacologically inert pills—when prescribed by the all-powerful physician indicates the enormous healing properties of emotions and attitudes that can be mobilized to operate in cases of painful and organic "diseases."

Christians like Pascal and Kierkegaard see faith as a "gamble," a "risk." Pascal's famous wager is that either God exists or he does not exist, and neither proposition can be proved. So we must wager. The odds are: if we wager that God exists and we are right, we win everything; if we are wrong we lose nothing. If you passed this up, "you would be imprudent."

But after all, God might punish those who wager on his existence. The Talmud does not generally approve of gambling.[11] Nietzsche remarked that when Kant wagered on God he became an idiot.[12] Competence in mathematics does not guarantee against pathetic fallacies in logic and religion. Pascal's God who protects those who wager prudently is not the God of the Patriarchs who risked everything on their faith. Pascal's wager is an escape from faith, especially blind faith, and rather resembles the experienced gambler who knows how to hedge bets and lay off risks till the odds against him are negligible. That such an individual should be accorded accolades of piety would come as a stunning surprise to the recipient. Indeed it might be the subject of a satiric musical comedy, "Guys and Gods," perhaps, or "A Horse Named Desire."

While logical verities are the hand-maiden of empirical science, belief offers not merely a guide to living, not a vehicle for entering into life, but life itself.

Notes

1. Julian Huxley, *Man in the Modern World* (New York: Mentor Books, 1948), p. 138.
2. Norman Kemp Smith, *A Commentary to Kant's "Critique of Pure Reason"* (New York: The Humanities Press, 1950), p. 23.
3. Ibid.
4. Georg Wilhelm Friedrich Hegel, *The Philosophy of History,* (New York: Dover Publications, 1956), p. 324.
5. Erwin R. Goodenough, *Religious Tradition and Myth,* (New Haven: Yale University Press, 1937), p. 58.
6. See Harry Austryn Wolfson, *Philo* (Cambridge: Harvard University Press, 1947). See also Wolfson, *The Philosophy of the Church Fathers* (Cambridge: Harvard University Press, 1956).
7. This philosophy originating with Philo dominated the thinking of the early Church Fathers through the Middle Ages till it was brought to an abrupt halt by Spinoza's *Theologico-Political Treatise* (1670), where the principle of causality replaces God. In short he denies the validity of revelation and returns to the classical

tradition of Greek philosophy in regarding reason as the paramount source of morality. See Wolfson, op cit., *Philo* Vol. II, p. 457. An account of Spinoza's blatant anti-Semitism is discussed in Leon Poliakov, *The History of Anti-Semitism* (New York: The Vanguard Press, Inc. 1973), Vol. II, pp. 268-278.
8. (New York: The Macmillan Company, 1931), p. 3
9. Sigmund Freud, *Civilization and its Discontents*, The Standard Edition (London: The Hogarth Press, 1961), Vol. XXI, p. 74.
10. (New York: Basic Books, Inc., 1965), p. 12.
11. Walter Kaufman, *Critique of Religion and Philosophy* (Garden City: Doubleday & Co., 1958), p. 171.

The Kingdom of God— Kosher Style

It may be a matter of some concern that the Hebrew word *Mashiah*, in Greek *Christos*, English *Messiah*, is an adjective, not a noun, meaning "anointed" (with oil). In the Hebrew Bible, kings and high priests are thus described for these were anointed with oil. The non-Hebrew king, Cyrus of Persia, is also referred to as anointed. There were the Patriarchs who may never have been physically anointed but who are called by this name. "Touch not mine anointed" (Ps. 105:15; I Chron 16:22). At times the word is universalized to include the whole people (Ps. 89:38, 51; 84:9).

Thus the word *Mashiah*, a term for anointed with oil, became an honorific title signifying "chosen", for the act of anointing was the sign of choice and elevation. The meaning was extended to include the expected redeemer of the future, chosen by God from birth, also called "Messiah." It is notable that this word "Messiah" does not occur in the Hebrew Bible, or even the Apocrypha. Thus the idea of savior and redeemer was not connected with the "anointing," but with the installation of king and high priest.

The belief in the Messiah of the people of Israel combines the political with the ethical. In Christianity the political and nationalistic have been sundered leaving only the ethical and spiritual.

The kingdom of the Jewish Messiah was never conceived as "a kingdom not of this world" (Jn. 18:36). The Messiah prepares a world for God's kingdom, but the world to be prepared is *this world*. Its Messiah was spiritual and political at the same time. The idea of the Messiah was an entirely original idea of Israel. No nation in the world knew a belief like this.

In the early period of Christianity the only distinction between the believers in Jesus and the Jews expecting the Messiah—the people of Antioch could find no more fitting name than "Christians"—derived from the Greek translation *(Chrestus)* of the Hebrew word "Messiah" (Mashiah) (Acts 11:26). At first the only difference was that Jews believed that the Messiah was *still to come* and the latter that the Messiah *had already come.*

Because of fear of Roman persecution of believers in a political Messiah, the Messiah of Christianity evolved into a symbol who did not come to redeem the sufferers of political and economic oppression but to redeem from spiritual evil alone. In Judaism Man must redeem himself from sin not by faith alone, but by repentance and good works.[1]

The institution of the Judges was one of original monotheistic creativity. It is a peculiarly Israelite expression of monotheism. Popular civil government by elders resembles a primitive democracy.

The authority of the elders yields to the authority of inspired men, the Judges. Its function even in Israel is confined to the early period and then disappears completely. There were no fixed forms or a political body but in times of national crisis an inspired man would arise, sent by God to save the people.[2] Among these Judges were Deborah and

Samuel, Gideon and Samson. But the spirit also seizes such as Jephthah, Othniel, and Ehud.

"I shall not rule over you," says Gideon to the people who have asked him to become king, "nor shall my sons rule over you; YHWH shall rule over you" (Judges 8:23).

The rule of inspired men continued for several generations. Since inspiration was a gift of God, and each instance a new act of grace, there could be no hereditary succession to judgeship. The institution is based upon faith in the election of Israel by the one God. YHWH manifested his kingship in Israel's history by sending it apostles to save it from oppression. The appearance of inspired saviors is proof of Israel's election of God's kingship. It was a period of rich creative activity. The "Kingdom of God" lasted for about 200 years (c. 1230 to 1024 BCE) to the founding of the monarchy.

Although Samuel made of his sons Judges the elders of Israel rejected them and asked for "a king to govern us like all the nations" (I Samuel 8:7). The Lord said "Hearken to the voice of the people—for they have not rejected you, but they have rejected me from being king over them" (I Samuel 8:7). Samuel opposes the request but he yields and anoints a king for them. This marks the monarchy as the direct successor of the "Kingdom of God." The first three kings of Israel are inspired with the spirit of YHWH and thus the kingdom of the "spirit" continues even after the prophetic "Kingdom of God" has passed away.

In Biblical literature the redeemer is God; in the extra canonical literature and the Rabbinic Aggada, he is the messianic king.[3] The image of the Messiah is two-fold: he is at once earthly and heavenly. He is the son of David and is expected to restore Israel's monarchy, at the same time he is a supernatural being who will establish the kingdom of God. Malachi 3:1 speaks of an angel who shall prepare the way—Elijah. According to Daniel 12:1, Michael the angel is to fill the role. These are the ideas that dominate early Christian writings.

Martin Buber puts the matter thus:

"Age after age the Jewish people believed in the Messianic tidings."

"If we consider all the reasons for anti-Semitism advanced by the Christian nations, we find that they are all superficial and transitory. But if we go deeper, we find that there is one deep and unconscious reason that is true for all periods of the Exile. It is that there has entered and become dispersed among them a people carrying a charge from heaven which is written in a book which became sacred for them too when they became Christians. It is unique in human history, strange and awesome, that heaven should make a specific demand in reference to human behavior, and that the demand should be recorded in a book, and that the book should be the heritage of a people that is dispersed among all the nations with this, its holy book, which is holy for all the nations as well. The demand hovers high over them as the comprehensive demand that their God makes of them.

"To be sure, they wish to retain the God they have received, but at the same time they would reject His demand. In so doing they rely upon the teachings of Saul, a Jew from Tarsus, who asserted that it was impossible to fulfill the demand and that it was necessary to cast off its yoke by submission to another Jew, Jesus of Nazareth, who had died during Saul's lifetime and was the Messiah, who had indeed fulfilled the demand and abolished it at the same time, who demanded nothing of his true believers save faith."

"Yet against all their opposition to the Torah stood that unfortunate Jewish people bearing the book which was its own book and at the same time part of the holy book of the nations. Their theologians argue that God rejected this people, who no longer have any heritage because that heritage has now passed over to Christianity. But the Jewish people continued to exist, book in hand; and even though they were burned at the stake, the words of the book were still on their lips. That is the perennial source of anti-Semitism.

"The peoples accepted the Gospel, but with it came the Torah of Israel, which comprehends three things: first the history of creation, which develops into the history of Israel; second the revelation of God, which was first of all His revelation to Israel; and third, the Messianic prophecy, whose center and focal point is the effort of Israel for the redemption of humanity." [4]

Notes

1. Joseph Klausner, *The Messianic Idea in Israel* (New York: The Macmillan Company, 1955), pp. 519, 531.
2. For the history of this period consult *The World History of the Jewish People*, Vol. III, "Judges". A. Malamat, ed. Benjamin Mazar. (Israel: Rutgers University Press, 1971), pp. 129-164.
3. Yehezkel Kaufmann, *Great Ages and Ideas of the Jewish People: The Biblical Age*, ed. Leo W. Schwarz (New York: Random House, 1956), p. 86.
4. Martin Buber, *On Judaism*, ed. Nahum N. Glatzer (New York: Schocken Books, 1967), pp. 184-187.

The Post-Christian Era

The post-Christian era means the end of Christian persecution of other faiths. "The claim for equal toleration with others which was advanced by the apologists in the days of their suffering, the Church did not grant to others in the days of her triumph." [1]

The very term "post-Christian" is ambiguous. It suggests a starting point, a realization of past faults and the possibility of new insights and strengthened relationships, such as a post-graduate climbing to a loftier peak than the mere graduate. This is not the case. The period in which Christianity was the dominating force is now at an end and one must take cognizance of the importance of this shattering alteration in the balance of world power and its change as it reflects the religious situation.

The Christian era did not start with the birth of Jesus but with the establishment of Christianity as the state religion of the Roman Empire by Constantine in the fourth century. Christianity did not flower in the Empire by the power of a religious idea but by the sword of the emperor.

As soon as Christianity was established it made haste to

declare Judaism an odious heretic sect and its propagation forbidden under the penalty of death. The violent conquest of Europe began. Europe was Christianized by the sword. When the power of secular rulers could no longer be denied, Innocent III devised the doctrine of the "Two Swords"—the Pope's and the Prince's—with the Pope's remaining superior.[2] It was heretical to suppose two co-equal vicars on earth. The argument of the two swords is cogent only if we take it for granted that God has destined both swords for the protection of the one and only church. The absorption of the State by the Church is proclaimed as a first principle by Gregory VII. Innocent III gave this doctrine the juristic shape in which it passed into the Canon Law. The Church has the spiritual and temporal power. The temporal as well as the spiritual power belongs to the chair of Peter and the separation affects only the administration, not the substance. The Pope notwithstanding, the office of the secular magistrate may directly interfere in temporal affairs. The plenitude of all power, worldly as well as spiritual, is committed to the Pope. The Pope has both swords and commits one of them to other hands merely for use. The Pope retained power to depose temporal rulers and free his subjects from the oath of fealty.

With the establishment of the church militant all other religions and heresies were exterminated.[3] Europe was converted to Christianity by force of military conquest. Saxons, Franks and aboriginal tribes were offered baptism or death. Christianity was established in Asia and Africa in the aggressive wake of the Western colonizing powers.

This era has come to a complete and final end. The dethronement of Western Europe from mastery of the globe does not mean that the era of Western dominance is past. There has been an unprecedented Westernized industrialization of all the peoples of the earth. At its apogee Western power operated with Bronze Age barbarianism and ruthless pugnacity. Its chief character was an unprecedented savage warlikeness.

The doctrine of the "two swords" has passed on to willing successors, Red China, the Soviets, Moslems, Hindus and Buddhists. They, the majority, now have the brute power that once was the monopoly of the Christian era.

This new realignment of power is recognized by the church in a spirit of ecumenism. The church once again affirms the principle of freedom of worship and conscience. As Arthur Cohen has put it: "The Christian comes to depend upon the Jew who says salvation has not yet come, to interpret for him what happens when power collapses, how men shall behave when the relative and conditional institutions of society crumble, for the Jew is an expert in unfulfilled time, whereas the Christian is an adept believer for redeemed times *only*."[4]

The Christian community born between the death of Jesus and the theology of Paul was not a continuation of the Jewish community. The new community had no history and traditional Judaism remained binding while preparation and ritual are introduced for the believer of the consummation.

This group at first was seen as a collection of Jewish heretics. The teaching of Paul had been making "proselytes" to Christianity. These were not proselytes in the Jewish Noachic sense, but the Church itself was still a Jewish sect in the minds of both Jews and Romans. Paul himself was still a Jew, and he was enunciating a doctrine that those who believed his teaching were the true Israel. The Christian New Covenant denies the legitimacy of Jewish existence. It grants them a negative role till the time when they shall admit their error and join the true Covenant of Israel, now passed on to its predestined heirs foretold in the Scriptures, the Christians.

The Second Vatican Council read as a whole, "the preponderant Christology expressed was one of fulfillment and absolute necessity for Christ as mediator of salvation. The Old Testament was most often understood primarily (although not exclusively) as preparatory to full consummation and flowering in Christianity, with Christ as the fulfillment of all Israel's hopes and prophecies." [5]

The largest number of Jews in the world are concentrated in the United States and this fact has not escaped the attention of the ecumenists. For many years the Lutheran Church in the United States has sought mutual understanding with the Jewish people. The initial result was the Evanston Report (1954) which begins with the assertion "Jesus Christ is the Savior of all mankind." The crux of that document claims that eventually all Jews must become Christian.[6]

Jacob Jocz, in a series of lectures at Princeton University (1965) on Jewish-Christian relationships, noted that for Christians to refrain from preaching Christ to the Jews is an act of unfaithfulness to the Christian message.[7]

Jean Danielou, the noted French Catholic theologian, said: "Neither is the Jewish religion on equal terms with Christianity, nor can we (Christians) give up trying to convert you (Jews)." [8]

Christ's claim is ultimate and Judaism's contemporary role quite subordinate. "We Christians cannot give up some kind of mission to the Jews because if we did, we would no longer be Church" (Joseph R. Estes).[9]

Eva Marie Fleishner, professor at Montclair State College, has even gone so far as to fish up a theological pluralism which would refrain from denying to the Jews freedom and identity and imposing on them the Christian version of truth. But even she admits that, on the final day, all people will be brought before Christ.[10]

The Council Fathers declared: "The principal purpose to which the plan of the Old Covenant was directed was to

prepare for the coming both of Christ, the universal Redeemer, and of the messianic kingdom, to announce this
coming by prophecy."

The recently formed Vatican Commission for Religious
Relations with Jews issued the official "Guidelines and Sug-
gestions" (1975):

"In view of her divine mission, and her very nature, the
Church must preach Jesus Christ to the world. While respecting religious freedom they (Christians) will strive to
understand the difficulties which arise for the Jewish
soul. . .when faced with the mystery of the incarnate
Word." [12]

Rabbi Eliezer Berkovitz presents a rejoinder [13]: "What
should be the Jewish attitude facing Christianity in the
post-Christian era of world history? For the first time since
the early days of the fourth century there may be a con-
frontation between Judaism and Christianity in freedom. In
this new type of encounter with Christianity our generation
must stand for all the generations that ever lived and suffered in Christian lands.

"In terms of the Jewish experience in the lands of Christendom, the final result of that age is bankruptcy—the
moral bankruptcy of the Christian religion. What was
started at the Council of Nicea was duly completed in the
concentration camps and the crematoria. [The Vatican
Council] has thought fit to declare solemnly before all the
world that the Jews are not to be considered a people accursed by God; the Jews are not collectively guilty for the
death of Jesus. For many centuries it was they who have
been doing the prosecuting, they who perpetuated abominable acts of inhumanity against the Jewish people, but
now they condescend to tell the world that we are perhaps
not guilty nor to be considered accursed by God. . . . To be
told after sixteen centuries of oppression and persecution in
Christian lands by those responsible for these acts of inhu-

manity that the Jews are not a people accursed by God is an offense not so much to Jews as to God.

"Many Christians and Jews are these days advocating the idea of a Jewish-Christian dialogue. On the level of philosophic thought, contact and interchange of ideas are certainly to be desired. . . . As to a dialogue in the purely theological sense, nothing could be more fruitless and pointless. Judaism is Judaism because it rejects Christianity and Christianity is Christianity because it rejects Judaism. What is usually referred to as the Judeo-Christian tradition exists only in Christian or secularist fancy. As far as Jews are concerned, Judaism is fully sufficient. There is nothing in Christianity for them. Whatever in Christian teaching is acceptable to them is borrowed from Judaism. Jews do not have to turn to the New Testament. Jesus was quoting from the Hebrew Bible. And whatever is not Jewish in Christianity is not acceptable to the Jew.

"There is a noteworthy contradiction as regards this matter of the fraternal dialogue in the pronouncements of the Vatican Council. On the one hand the council encourages dialogues with other religions; on the other, it also affirms that the Roman Catholic Church is the only repository of all true religion. What then is the purpose of the dialogue for the Church? There is nothing that Christianity may gain by it.

"However, independently of all considerations of inter-religious politics, we reject the idea of inter-religious understanding on ethical grounds. First of all, it represents a distortion of historic truth; it is a falsification of the true nature of the Judeo-Christian tragedy. It suggests a measure of mutuality in the responsibility for that tragedy; as if there had been friction and conflict because we did not know each other well enough; as if there had been struggle between Jews and Christians because they were not familiar with each other's noble religious traditions and beliefs. This is not the case. There were no conflicts or wars. There was only unilateral oppression and persecution. We reject the idea of inter-religious understanding as immoral because it is an attempt to whitewash a criminal past.

"All we want of Christians is that they keep their hands off us and our children! Human beings ought to treat each other with respect and hold each other dear independently of theological dialogues, Biblical studies, and independently of what they believe about each other's religion. I am free to reject any religion as humbug if that is what I think of it; but I am duty-bound to respect the dignity of every human being no matter what I may think of his religion. It is not inter-religious understanding that mankind needs but inter-*human* understanding.

"We who were there when the Christian era began; we in whose martyrdom Christianity suffered its worst moral debacle; we in whose blood the Christian era found its end—we are here as this new era opens. And we shall be here when this new era reaches its close—we—God's own witnesses—the eternal witness of history."

The events of this century are too vast to be comprehended and anything we say must be considered partial or trite. But the notion of erecting a spiritual ghetto to replace the iron gates of Auschwitz is precisely wrong, unwise, if not sinful. To know the right thing to do we need to know what the social situation is now. Moral judgments institute a relationship between persons, and relationships between persons constitute society. It is an error to suppose that society can consist of a number of noninterracting fields. Without the attempt to formulate and restate ideas in common we are kept in the domain of opinion and conflict. We need the formulation of new commitments beyond special interests and tradition.

Ability to develop a changed mode of adaptation in response to new conditions is what enabled the Jewish community to survive successive waves of discrimination. When ideas become final they become apologetics or propaganda. We live in a world of process in which the future, although continuous with the past, is not its bare repetition. The value of ideas lies in what proceeds from them, not their antecedents.

Plato defined a slave as one who accepts from another the purposes which control his conduct. Our aim must always represent a freeing of activities. When we have reached a turning point our activities will need redirection. The termination of the present mode means the beginning of a new one. Ends are beginnings.

It is the experience of shared concerns that becomes common knowledge. The secular anti-Semitism of the left is today the most virulent opponent of freedom for Jews.

Mirabeau in his efforts to secure the rights of Frenchmen for Jews made the point that the Jew is more of a man than he is a Jew. The point was forcibly put: "One must refuse everything to the Jews as a nation, but one must give them everything as individuals; they must become citizens."

This was less of a demand than a description of an ongoing process. In the context of these ideas the term *man* meant an individual who had abandoned superstitions and prejudices for reason and light. Those who helped to emancipate the Jews had some vision of what they ought to be made to become. The great difference between the Jewish experience in America and France was that their right to participate in the new order in France was made conditional on their becoming "new men." The new Jew was never told exactly what he had to prove and this is reflected in the parables of Kafka.

"Jesus was born among Jews on Jewish soil, and his message was for Jews alone. In its origin, therefore, and in so far as it is dependent on its traditional founder, Christianity must be considered a Jewish phenomenon." So Charles

Guignebert opens his great work, *The Jewish World in the Time of Jesus.*[14]

While Christianity may thus be considered a daughter religion of Judaism, it is a peculiar daughter that seeks to devour and destroy its mother. In replying to Rabbi Berkovitz, I do not gloss over the usurpation of the Hebrew Bible, the hostility and unparalleled animosity to the Jews in the official canon of the Christian religion, the pogroms, mass expulsions, inquisitions, forced baptism, the auto-da-fé, blood accusations, host desecrations, the Crusades, the Black Death, modern national anti-Semitism culminating in the Holocaust, Hitler's personal legacy in the post-war hatred and pogroms in Eastern Europe and Soviet and Arab plans for the destruction of Israel. Nor do I forget the policy of indifference and hostility of Western nations to the plight of Jews seeking refuge from Hitler's terror and later all occupied Europe. Even a diplomatic protest, a moral outcry might have stayed the Bloody Hand and brought hope to millions. Many officials among the Allies could well have stood in the dock at Nuremberg with the Nazi leaders for making possible the success of the conspiracy to murder the Jewish peoples of the world.

Yet when Michael B. McGarry, author of *Christology After Auschwitz,* writes: "If Jews are no longer the object of a conversationist program (as many Christians concede), if they are partners in a dialogue, then the new dialogical relation between the faiths presupposes some sort of equality where each has something to contribute to the other, and, more telling, where each lacks something which only the other can contribute," [15] I say it is a fair statement.

Notes

1. James Parkes, *The Conflict of the Church and the Synagogue* (Cleveland and New York: World Publishing Company, 1961), p. 157.
2. Otto Gierke, *Political Theories of the Middle Ages*, tr. F.W. Maitland. (Boston: Beacon Press, 1960), p. 113.
3. See Zoe Oldenbourg, *Massacre at Montsegur* (New York: Minerva Press, 1968). "On 10th March 1208 His Holiness Pope Innocent III issued a solemn call to arms, summoning all Christian nations to launch a crusade against a country of fellow-Christians" (p. 1). It was not heresy they were called upon to fight so much as a region largely sympathetic towards heresy and giving protection to Jews. See also Henry Charles Lea, *The Inquisition of the Middle Ages* (New York: The Citadel Press, 1961).
4. Arthur A. Cohen, *The Myth of the Judeo-Christian Tradition* (New York: Schocken Books, 1971), p. XX.
5. Michael B. McGarry, C.S.P., *Christology After Auschwitz* (New York: Paulist Press, 1977), p. 27.
6. Ibid., p. 60.

  7. Ibid., pp. 64, 65.
  8. Ibid., p. 67.
  9. Ibid., p. 70.
10. Ibid., p. 75.
11. Ibid., p. 19.
12. Ibid., p. 38.
13. *Disputation and Dialogue,* ed. F.E. Talmage. Eliezer Berkovits, *Judaism in the Post-Christian Era* (New York: KTAV Publishing House Inc., 1975), pp. 284-295.
14. (New Hyde Park: University Books, 1959), p. 1.
15. Michael B. McGarry, op. cit., p. 10.

Bibliography

Allegro, John M., *The Sacred Mushroom and the Cross.* London, Hodder and Stoughton, 1970.

———. *The Dead Sea Scrolls.* Middlesex, Penguin Books, Ltd. 1956.

———. *The Chosen People.* New York, Doubleday & Co., Inc. 1971.

Althusius, Johannes, The Politics of Johannes Althusius, tr. and ed. by Frederick S. Carney. London, Eyre & Spottiswoode, 1965.

Arendt, Hannah, *Antisemitism.* New York, Harcourt, Brace & World, 1951.

Augstein, Rudolf. *Jesus Son of Man.* New York, Urizen Books, 1977.

Baeck, Leo, *The Essence of Judaism.* New York, Schocken Books, 1948.

Barnes, Harry Elmer, *Sociology and Political Theory.* New York, A.A. Knopf, 1924.

Berkovits, Eliezer, *Judaism in the Post-Christian Era. Disputation and Dialogue,* ed. F.E. Talmage. New York, KTAV Publishing House, Inc. 1975.

Berry, Lester V. and Van Den Bark, Melvin, *The American*

Thesaurus of Slang. New York, Thomas Y. Crowell Company, 1942.

Blumenkranz, B., *The Dark Ages.* Cecil Roth, ed. New Brunswick, Rutgers University Press, 1966.

Brandon, S.G.F., *The Judgment of the Dead.* New York, Charles Scribner's Sons, 1967.

———. *Jesus and the Zealots.* Manchester, Charles Scribner's Sons, 1967.

———. *The Fall of Jerusalem and the Christian Church.* London, S.P.C.K., 1974.

Buber, Martin, *Two Types of Faith.* New York, Harper & Row, 1961.

———. *On Judaism,* ed. Nahum N. Glazer. New York, Schocken Books, 1967.

Cohane, John Phillip, *The Key.* New York, Schocken Books, 1976.

Cohen, Arthur A., *The Myth of the Judeo-Christian Tradition.* New York, Schocken Books, 1971.

Cohen, Morris Raphael, *Reason and Law.* New York, Collier Books, 1961.

Cohn, Haim, *The Trial and Death of Jesus.* New York, Harper & Row, 1971.

Cohn, Norman, *Warrant for Genocide.* New York, Harper & Row, 1966.

Coulton, G.G., *Medieval Panorama.* New York, Meridian Books, 1955.

———. *Medieval Village, Manor, and Monastery.* New York, Harper and Brothers, 1960.

Cumont, Franz, *The Mysteries of Mithra.* New York, Dover Publications, Inc., 1956.

Daube, David, *The New Testament and Rabbinic Judaism.* London, The Athlone Press, 1956.

Davies, A. Powell, *The Meaning of the Dead Sea Scrolls.* New York, The New American Library, 1956.

Davies, W.D., *The Setting of the Sermon on the Mount.* Cambridge, Cambridge University Press, 1963.

Eckhardt, A. Roy, *Elder and Younger Brothers.* New York, Schocken Books, 1973.

————. *Your People, My People.* New York, Quadrangle, 1974.

Eckhardt, Alice and Roy, *Encounter with Israel.* New York, Association Press, 1970.

Fichte, Johann Gottlieb, *Addresses to the German Nation.* George A. Kelley, ed., New York, Harper & Row, 1968.

Flannery, Edward H., *The Anguish of the Jews.* New York, The Macmillan Company, 1965.

Freud, Sigmund, Standard Edition, Vol XIV, London, The Hogarth Press, 1957.

————. *Civilization and its Discontents.* The Standard Edition, London, The Hogarth Press, Vol. XXI, 1961.

Gierke, Otto, *Natural Law and the Theory of Society.* tr. Ernest Barker, Cambridge, Cambridge University Press. Reprinted Boston, Beacon Press, 1960.

————. *Political Theories of the Middle Age.* tr. F.W. Maitland, Boston, Beacon Press, 1960.

Gobineau, Count Arthur de, *Selected Political Writings.* Michael D. Biddiss, ed. London, Jonathan Cape, 1970.

Goodenough, Erwin R., *The Psychology of Religious Experiences.* New York, Basic Books, Inc., 1965.

————. *Religious Tradition and Myth.* New Haven, Yale University Press, 1937.

Gordon, Cyrus H., *The Common Background of Greek and Hebrew Civilization.* New York, W.W. Norton & Company, Inc., 1965.

————. *The Ancient Near East.* New York, W.W. Norton & Company, Inc., 1965.

Grant, Frederick C., *Ancient Judaism and the New Testament.* New York, The Macmillan Company, 1959.

Grant, Michael, *Jesus An Historian's Review of the Gospels.* New York, Charles Scribner's Sons, 1977.

Graves, Robert and Podro, Joshua, *The Nazarene Gospel*

Restored. New York, Doubleday and Company, 1954.

Guignebert, Charles, *Jesus.* New York, University Books, 1956.

———. *The Jewish World in the Time of Jesus.* New Hyde Park, University Books, 1959.

Hadas, Moses and Smith, Morton, *Heroes and Gods.* New York, Harper and Row, 1965.

Hall, Jerome, *Readings in Jurisprudence.* Indianapolis, The Bobbs-Merrill Company, 1938.

Hatch, Edwin. *The Influence of Greek Ideas on Christianity.* New York, Harper and Brothers, 1957.

Hay, Malcom, *The Brother's Blood.* New York, Hart Publishing Company, 1965.

Hegel, Georg Wilhelm Friedrich, *The Philosophy of History,* tr. J. Sibree. New York, Dover Publications, 1956.

Herder, Johann Gottfried von, *Reflections on the Philosophy of the History of Mankind,* tr. Frank E. Mannel. Chicago, The University of Chicago Press, 1968.

Herford, R. Traverse, *The Pharisees.* Boston, Beacon Press, 1962.

Huxley, Julian, *Man in the Modern World.* New York, Mentor Books, 1948.

Isaac, Jules, *The Teaching of Contempt.* New York, Holt, Rinehart, and Winston, 1964.

———. *Jesus and Israel.* New York, Holt, Rinehart and Winston, 1971.

Jeans, Sir James, *The Mysterious Universe.* New York, The Macmillan Company, 1931.

Kaufmann, Walter, *Critique of Religion and Philosophy.* Garden City, Doubleday and Company, 1958.

Kaufmann, Yehezkel, *The Biblical Age, Great Ages and Ideas of the Jewish People,* ed. Leo W. Schwarz. New York, Random House, 1956.

Kee, Howard Clark, *Jesus in History.* New York, Harcourt, Brace and World, Inc. 1970.

Kierkegaard, Søren, *Training in Christianity.* Walter

Lowrie, tr. Princeton, Princeton University Press, 1944.

Klausner, Joseph, *The Messianic Idea in Israel.* New York, The Macmillan Company, 1955.

Kohn, Hans, *Prophets and Peoples.* London, Collier-Macmillan Ltd., 1961.

―――. *Political Ideologies of the Twentieth Century.* 3rd Ed. Rev., New York, Harper and Row, 1966.

―――. *The Mind of Germany.* New York, Harper and Row, 1960.

Lamont, Corliss, ed. *Dialogue on John Dewey.* New York, Horizon Press, 1959.

Lea, Henry Charles, *The Inquisition of the Middle Ages.* New York, The Citadel Press, 1961.

Lehmann, Johannes, *Rabbi J.* New York, Stein and Day, 1971.

Maccoby, Hyam, *Revolution in Judaea, Jesus, and the Jewish Heritage.* New York, Taplinger Publishing Company, 1980.

Maitland, Frederic William, *The Deacon and the Jewess; or Apostasy at Common Law.* 2 Law Quarterly Review 153, 1886. Reprinted in *Landmarks of Law.* Ray D. Henson, ed. Boston, Beacon Press, 1963.

―――. *Political Theories of the Middle Age.* London, Cambridge University Press, 1900. Reprinted Boston, Beacon Press, 1958.

―――. *Roman Canon Law in the Church of England.* London, Methuen and Company, 1898.

―――. *Selected Historical Essays of F.W. Maitland.* Helen M. Cam, ed. Boston, Beacon Press, 1962.

―――. *The Letters of Frederic William Maitland.* C.H.S. Fifoot, ed. London, Cambridge University Press, 1965.

Mazar, Benjamin, *Judges. The World History of the Jewish People.* Vol. III., ed. A. Malamat. Israel, Rutgers University Press, 1971.

McGarry, Michael G., *Christology After Auschwitz.* New York, Paulist Press, 1977.

Miller, Jr., Orson K. *Mushrooms of North America.* New York, E.P. Dutton and Co., Inc., 1972.

Mosse, George L., *The Crisis of German Ideology.* New York, Grosset and Dunlap, 1964.

Murray, James A.H. *et al. The Oxford English Dictionary.* Glasgow, Oxford University Press, 1971.

Nietzsche, Friedrich, *Beyond Good and Evil.* tr. Walter Kaufmann. New York, Vintage Books, 1966.

Oldenbourg, Zoe, *Massacre at Montsegur.* New York, Minerva Press, 1968.

Parkes, James, *The Foundations of Judaism and Christianity.* Chicago, Quadrangle Books, 1960.

———. *The Conflict of the Church and the Synagogue.* Cleveland and New York, The World Publishing Company, 1961.

Poliakov, Leon, *The History of Anti-Semitism,* Vol. I, New York, Schocken Books, 1974.

———. *The History of Anti-Semitism,* Vol. II. New York, The Vanguard Press, Inc., 1973.

Polish, David, *The Higher Freedom.* Chicago, Quadrangle Books, 1965.

Pollock, Frederick and Maitland, Frederic W., *The History of English Law.* London, Cambridge University Press, 1968.

Ramsbottom, John, *Mushrooms and Toadstools.* London, Collins, 1953.

Richardson, Cyril C., ed., Hardy, E.R. tr., *Early Christian Fathers.* New York, The Macmillan Company, 1970.

Rubenstein, Richard L., *The Religious Imagination.* Boston, Beacon Press, 1971.

Schechter, Solomon, *Studies in Judaism.* New York, Meridian Books, Inc., 1958.

Schwarz, Leo W., *Wolfson of Harvard.* Philadelphia, The Jewish Publication Society of America, 1978.

Shiel, James, *Greek Thought and the Rise of Christianity.* New York, Barnes & Noble, Inc., 1968.

Silver, Abba Hillel, *Where Judaism Differed.* New York, The Macmillan Company, 1956.

Smith, Morton, *Clement of Alexandria and a Secret Gospel of Mark.* Cambridge, Harvard University Press, 1973.

————. *Jesus The Magician.* New York, Harper & Row, 1978.

Smith, Norman Kemp, *A Commentary to Kant's 'Critique of Pure Reason.'* New York, The Humanities Press, 1950.

Spinoza, Benedict de, *A Theologico-Political Treatise,* tr. R.H.M. Elwes. New York, Dover Publications, Inc., 1951.

Stern, M. *The World History of the Jewish People.* Michael Avi-Yonah, ed. Vol. VII. New Brunswick, Rutgers University Press, 1975.

Wiener, Philip P. *et al.* ed. *Dictionary of the History of Ideas.* Vol. III. New York, Charles Scribner's Sons, 1973.

Winter, Paul, *On the Trial of Jesus.* Berlin, Walter De Gruyter and Company, 1961.

Wolfson, Harry Austryn, *Philo,* Cambridge, Harvard University Press, 1947.

————. *The Philosophy of the Church Fathers.* Cambridge, Harvard University Press, 1956.

Collective Works Consulted

The Jewish Encyclopedia, 12 Vol. New York, Funk & Wagnalls Company, 1901.

The Talmud, Rabbi Dr. I. Epstein, tr. & ed. London, The Soncino Press, 1935-1952. 18 Vol. Ed.